We've taken liberties with the translations in this book! Here are variations on the conventional stir-fry that you might never have imagined but, once you discover how surprisingly easy they are to make and how wonderfully delicious, will want to make time and time again... breaking with tradition to make new "old favourites". Plus, I hope when you realise what latitude you have with wok cookery, you'll be fast frying your own creations.

Pamela Clark

FOOD EDITOR

the seasoned wok

The Seasoned Wok...

The success of our previous *Sensational Stir-Fries* indicated that you'd like this second serving of quick, delicious and healthy recipes which can be cooked in a wok – and, with *The Seasoned Wok*, we've added ease of preparation and innovative ideas into the mix. Stir in a batch of tips and techniques, add more-than-100 exciting recipes all pictured in colour, then combine to make *The Seasoned Wok* your most valuable kitchen tool.

Teriyaki beef with toasted nori and sesame, page 25

Crispy duck and creamy spinach risotto, page 65

Asparagus with citrus-toasted breadcrumbs, page 89

Hot and sticky ribs, page 17

Prawns in basil with avocado mash, page 76

Contents

BRITISH & NORTH AMERICAN READERS:
Please note that Australian cup and spoon measurements are metric. A quick conversion guide appears on page 119. A glossary explaining unfamiliar terms and ingredients begins on page 112.

Learning to wok

One of the most important components of stir-fry cooking is the perfectly seasoned wok – here's how to find the one that suits you best and produces the tastiest of meals.

Stir-frying is a simple, fast and healthy way to cook. Simple because, generally speaking, most of the preparation is done before you turn to the stove; fast because once you've heated your wok, it's usually only a few minutes before you're serving the food; and, last but probably most important, healthy because of the fast cooking time – the food you serve will still contain a great many of its original nutrients.

Choosing a wok

Woks come in a variety of sizes and finishes, ranging from the traditional carbon-steel wok to cast-iron, stainless-steel, forge-cast or anodised aluminium, non-stick and even electric woks. Traditional round-base woks are great for gas burners, while flat-base woks are well suited for electric stove elements. There are woks with lips, woks with a single long handle, woks with built-in "tempura" racks, woks as part of cook-tops. They range in diameter from 25cm (10 inches) to 60cm (24 inches) – and beyond, as seen in Chinese restaurant kitchens. Here, we've pictured a handful of the many woks most readily available from Asian food shops and most department or kitchen specialty stores.

Seasoning your wok

Carbon-steel and cast-iron woks must be "seasoned" (readied for cooking) before they're used for the first time. First, wash your wok in hot soapy water to remove all traces of grease, then dry it thoroughly. Place the wok on the stove over high heat; when hot, rub about 1 tablespoon of cooking oil over all of the inside surface with absorbent paper. Continue heating the wok for about 10 minutes, wiping from time to time with a ball of clean absorbent paper. This treatment creates a certain amount of smoke because you're effectively "burning off" the oil: make certain you're holding both the wok and the paper you're wiping it with wearing oven gloves. Repeat this whole process twice: your wok is now ready to use.

Its smooth, round "bowl" shape makes a wok quite easy to clean. Every time you use it, wash your wok in hot soapy water with a sponge, cloth or similar – never scrub it with scourers, steel-wool or harsh abrasives. Dry the wok thoroughly by placing it on the stove over low heat for a few minutes. Rub or spray a thin layer of cooking oil all over the inside of its bowl before storing your wok – to avoid rust. With constant use and care, your well-seasoned wok will reward you with years of service: the more used, more seasoned your wok becomes, the better it is as a cooking tool.

Woks (*clockwise from top left*) are: stainless-steel, with a tempura rack; anodised aluminium, with a flat base; carbon steel, on a wok burner; enamel-coated cast iron with a non-stick heavy-gauge carbon steel single-handled wok placed inside it. Two wok lids, one aluminium and one glass, are also shown.

Stir-frying accessories

Wooden tongs are used to turn foods cooking in a wok with a coated surface.

A **wok spatula**, or **chan**, is a long-handled, metal mini-shovel used to lift, toss and stir food. Invest in a wooden chan if you use a treated-surface non-stick wok, so that you don't scratch its surface.

A **tempura rack** comes in handy when used to drain foods that are deep-fried, in batches, in your wok.

One essential kitchen tool for ease and precision in cutting food to be stir-fried is a solid hardwood non-painted **chopping board**.

Wooden chopsticks help pick up selected small food bits from a wok.

Obviously you should possess either a **cleaver** or a very sharp knife to cut or chop the various ingredients you're using to the required size.

Steamer baskets made of bamboo can be stac one on top of another and are good when mak dim sum or gow gees: the steam passes thro the strips of bamboo, leaving the basket interi and your dough – condensation-f

When using your wok for shallow- or deep-frying, **metal tongs** are useful for lifting pieces of food in and out of the wok; they also help single out items that need to be turned.

A **wok burner** (or wok-hole for a barbecue) is a perforated metal ring that holds the wok securely and focuses the heat's intensity – a must for stir-frying.

It's a good idea to get a **high-domed** that fits your wok securely so steam circulates and doesn't esc during cooking ti

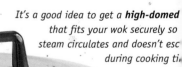

The right sauce

Pictured right are 14 of this book's most frequently called for sauces, vinegars, oils, etc, to help you to identify them on your next trip to the store. Be aware of the fact that, since there are many different types and labels found both in an average supermarket and in speciality food shops, you may not find the exact brands of the products we've selected here; these were chosen simply because they were generic and made in the country from which each one originally hails.

1. Peanut oil

2. Cider vinegar

3. Extra virgin olive oil

4. Balsamic vinegar

5. Raspberry vinegar

6. Sesame oil

7. Mirin

8. Soy sauce

9. Oyster sauce

10. Tahini

11. Tabasco sauce (mild)

12. Chinese cooking wine

13. Fish sauce

14. Tabasco sauce (hot)

Marinating food beforehand

• When marinating uncooked meat, poultry and seafood, any leftover marinade you intend to use in a sauce or dressing has to be brought to the boil before serving.

• Always cover and refrigerate all mixtures while they are marinating, regardless of what they may contain.

• Bottled sauces, marinades, pastes, etc, should be stored, lids on securely, in the refrigerator after opening.

Preparation techniques for stir-frying

Chilli 1. Care must be taken when handling chillies: wear rubber gloves. Wash hands, knife and chopping board thoroughly after use. Take care not to touch your eyes while handling chillies. **2.** Cut lengthways in half, scrape out seeds and membrane with the tip of a small knife. Flatten, skin-side down, on chopping board; cut into thin strips. Hold strips firmly together and chop.

Leek Trim away tough green leaves and root end; use only the white part of the leek. Leeks usually contain grit, so halve lengthways and wash under cold water to remove grit before slicing into thin strips. (Leek can also be cut in the same way as the green onion at right.)

Green onion Cut off the dark green stem tops and root. Peel off the first layer of the white bulb portion. Cut onion in half lengthways, then into 5cm lengths, then into thin strips.

Meat For best results, wrap meat tightly in plastic wrap, then partially freeze before cutting it into wafer-thin slices across the grain.

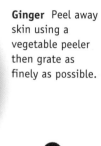

Ginger Peel away skin using a vegetable peeler then grate as finely as possible.

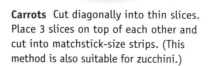

Asparagus Snap off the fibrous end of each spear. Using a vegetable peeler, scrape away nodules from the ends (not tips) of spears.

Carrots Cut diagonally into thin slices. Place 3 slices on top of each other and cut into matchstick-size strips. (This method is also suitable for zucchini.)

Lemon grass Remove and discard tough end and root. Quarter lengthways then holding firmly, chop finely.

Leafy gr
chopped
complet
residual
"cook",
pea spro

Onion **1.** Cut onion in half lengthways; peel and discard tough outer skin. Place, cut-side down, on chopping board; hold onion at root end, slice as finely as required. **2.** Place, cut-side down, on chopping board; cut into wedges. **3.** Place, cut-side down, on chopping board; make 1 or 2 horizontal cuts, making sure root end remains intact. Hold onion as shown, then make a series of vertical cuts without cutting through the root end. Hold onion firmly at root end; chop as finely as required (discard root end).

Garlic **1.** Crush garlic with the flat side of a large knife to loosen the skin, then peel the skin from the clove. **2.** Place peeled clove in garlic crusher, squeeze the handles together to force the garlic through the holes. Alternatively, place sliced peeled clove on a chopping board with a pinch of salt. Using the broad part of a knife blade, mash garlic by pushing the knife away from you.

Capsicum **1.** Halve crossways. Discard stem, seeds and membrane. **2.** Cut lengthways in half, place, skin-side down, on a board; press down to flatten. Cut lengthways into thin strips; hold strips firmly together and chop as desired.

1

2

3

Classics with a twist

These traditional stir-fry recipes are given a new lease on life by a cunning combination of the use of easy-to-find ingredients and the incorporation of timesaving techniques. This soup, for instance, is vegetarian bliss: get tofu at the supermarket, shiitake mushrooms and choy-sum from your greengrocer (or try button mushrooms and spinach); chop and stir-fry these with a little chilli and soy sauce, then add a package of vegetable stock. Heat and eat this classy classic soup, made from scratch in minutes.

SPICY BEEF AND VEGETABLES

700g beef steak, sliced thinly
1/4 teaspoon five-spice powder
1/3 cup (80ml) black bean sauce
1/3 cup (80ml) oyster sauce
1 clove garlic, crushed
4 bird's-eye chillies, seeded,
  chopped finely
85g instant noodles
1 tablespoon peanut oil
1 medium (150g) brown
  onion, sliced
2 medium (240g) carrots, chopped
565g can bamboo shoot slices,
  drained, chopped
150g snow peas, sliced

• Combine beef, five-spice, sauces, garlic and chilli in medium bowl, cover; refrigerate 3 hours or overnight.

To cook Cook noodles in medium pan of boiling water, uncovered, until just tender; drain.

• Heat oil in wok; stir-fry beef mixture and onion, in batches, until beef is browned.

• Stir-fry carrot in same wok until just tender and browned lightly.

• Return beef mixture to wok with bamboo shoots, snow peas and noodles; stir-fry, tossing to combine ingredients.

SERVES 4

Bowl from Accoutrement

LAKSA-FLAVOURED PRAWNS AND HOKKIEN NOODLES

450g Hokkien noodles
750g medium uncooked prawns
1 tablespoon peanut oil
2 medium (300g) white
  onions, sliced
2 cloves garlic, crushed
2 teaspoons grated fresh ginger
210g jar laksa paste
1²/3 cups (400ml) coconut cream
1 cup (250ml) vegetable stock
1 cup (80g) bean sprouts
2 tablespoons lime juice
2 tablespoons chopped fresh
  coriander leaves
2 green onions, chopped

• Rinse noodles under hot water; drain. Transfer to large bowl; separate noodles with fork.

• Shell and devein prawns, leaving tails intact. Heat oil in wok; stir-fry prawns, white onion, garlic and ginger, in batches, until prawns are changed in colour.

• Stir-fry laksa paste in same wok until fragrant and hot.

• Return prawn mixture to wok with cream, stock, sprouts, juice and noodles; stir-fry, tossing until sauce boils.

• Serve laksa sprinkled with coriander and green onion.

SERVES 4

HOT AND STICKY RIBS

1.5kg pork spareribs, chopped
2 tablespoons peanut oil
2 cloves garlic, crushed
2 teaspoons grated fresh ginger
2 tablespoons honey
1/3 cup (80ml) sweet chilli sauce
2 tablespoons plum sauce
2 teaspoons sambal oelek
1 tablespoon brown sugar
1 tablespoon chopped fresh
   coriander leaves

• Cook spareribs in large pan of boiling water, uncovered, about 10 minutes or until just cooked; drain spareribs, discard cooking liquid.

• Heat oil in wok; stir-fry spareribs, in batches, until browned and cooked as desired.

• Return spareribs to wok with combined remaining ingredients; stir-fry, tossing until sauce boils.

SERVES 4

Left Laksa-flavoured prawns and Hokkien noodles
Below Spicy beef and vegetables
Right Hot and sticky ribs

GINGERED PORK

700g pork fillets, sliced thinly
2 kaffir lime leaves, sliced thinly
2 tablespoons grated fresh ginger
1/4 cup chopped fresh
  coriander leaves
2 tablespoons peanut oil
1 medium (150g) white
  onion, sliced
1 medium (200g) yellow
  capsicum, sliced
1 medium (200g) red
  capsicum, sliced
2 tablespoons soy sauce
2 tablespoons rice vinegar
3 cups (240g) bean sprouts

• Combine pork, lime leaves, ginger and coriander in medium bowl, cover; refrigerate 3 hours or overnight.

To cook Heat oil in wok; stir-fry pork mixture and onion, in batches, until pork is browned and cooked as desired.

• Stir-fry capsicums in same wok until just tender and browned lightly.

• Return pork mixture to wok; stir in soy sauce and vinegar.

• Add sprouts; stir-fry, tossing until sprouts are just wilted.

SERVES 4

LAMB WITH SPRING ONIONS

700g lamb eye of loin, sliced thinly
4cm piece fresh ginger, sliced
4cm piece fresh lemon grass, sliced
2 cloves garlic, crushed
2 teaspoons grated lemon rind
1 tablespoon lemon juice
2 tablespoons peanut oil
400g (about 8) spring onions,
  trimmed, sliced
1/4 cup (60ml) sweet chilli sauce
1/2 teaspoon sesame oil
1 tablespoon dry sherry

• Combine lamb, ginger, lemon grass, garlic, rind and juice in medium bowl, cover; refrigerate 3 hours or overnight.

To cook Heat peanut oil in wok; stir-fry lamb mixture and onion, in batches, until lamb is browned.

• Add combined sauce, sesame oil and sherry; cook until sauce boils.

• Return lamb mixture to wok; stir-fry, tossing to combine with sauce.

SERVES 4

Above Gingered pork
Right Lamb with spring onions

FIVE-SPICE CHICKEN

**700g single chicken breast fillets,
sliced thinly**
1 teaspoon finely grated lime rind
2 tablespoons lime juice
2 cloves garlic, crushed
2 teaspoons grated fresh ginger
1 teaspoon five-spice powder
¼ cup (60ml) soy sauce
2 tablespoons peanut oil
**½ (about 250g) Chinese
cabbage, shredded**
1½ cups (120g) bean sprouts
8 green onions, sliced
**¼ cup loosely packed fresh
coriander leaves**

• Combine chicken, rind, juice, garlic,
ginger, five-spice and 1 tablespoon of the
soy sauce in large bowl, cover; refrigerate
3 hours or overnight.

To cook Heat ½ of the oil in wok; stir-
fry chicken mixture, in batches, until
chicken is browned and cooked through.

• Heat remaining oil in same wok; stir-fry
cabbage, sprouts and onion until cabbage
is just wilted.

• Return the chicken mixture to wok
with coriander and remaining soy sauce;
stir-fry, tossing to combine with the
vegetables. Serve with deep-fried rice
vermicelli, if desired.

SERVES 4

MIXED MUSHROOMS,
SPINACH AND BEEF

700g beef steak, sliced thinly
2 tablespoons oyster sauce
2 cloves garlic, crushed
2 tablespoons peanut oil
**250g shiitake mushrooms,
quartered**
250g oyster mushrooms
250g enoki mushrooms
250g baby spinach leaves

• Combine beef, oyster sauce and garlic
in large bowl, cover; refrigerate 3 hours
or overnight.

To cook Heat oil in wok; stir-fry beef
mixture, in batches, until browned.

• Stir-fry shiitake mushrooms in same wok
until just browned.

• Return beef to wok with remaining
mushrooms and spinach; stir-fry, tossing
until spinach is just wilted.

SERVES 4

Left Five-spice chicken
Right Mixed mushrooms, spinach and beef

BLACK BEAN AND SQUID STIR-FRY

10 medium (850g) squid
    hoods, chopped
1/2 cup (125ml) black bean sauce
1/4 cup (60ml) oyster sauce
2 tablespoons dry sherry
4 cloves garlic, crushed
1 tablespoon peanut oil
2 medium (400g) red
    capsicums, chopped
4 green onions, chopped finely
500g spinach, chopped

• Combine squid, sauces, sherry and garlic in large bowl, cover; refrigerate 1 hour.

To cook Drain squid over medium bowl; reserve marinade.

SWEET CHILLI CHICKEN WITH CASHEWS

700g single chicken breast fillets,
    sliced thinly
1/4 cup finely chopped fresh
    coriander leaves
2 bird's-eye chillies, seeded,
    chopped finely
1 tablespoon sesame oil
1 clove garlic, crushed
2 tablespoons peanut oil
1/3 cup (80ml) rice vinegar
1/4 cup (60ml) sweet chilli sauce
1 tablespoon lime juice
3/4 cup (105g) raw cashews, toasted
1 cup (80g) snow pea sprouts

• Combine chicken, coriander, chilli, sesame oil and garlic in large bowl, cover; refrigerate 3 hours or overnight.

To cook Heat peanut oil in wok; stir-fry chicken mixture, in batches, until browned and cooked through.

• Return chicken mixture to wok. Add vinegar, sauce and juice; stir-fry until sauce boils.

• Add cashews; stir-fry, tossing to combine with chicken mixture.

• Just before serving, gently toss sprouts with chicken mixture.

SERVES 4

- Heat oil in wok; stir-fry squid, in batches, until tender.

- Stir-fry capsicum and onion in same wok until onion is browned lightly.

- Return squid to wok with reserved marinade; stir-fry until sauce boils.

- Add spinach; stir-fry, tossing until spinach is just wilted.

SERVES 4 TO 6

Left Sweet chilli chicken with cashews
Centre Black bean and squid stir-fry
Right Lentil, pumpkin and spinach curry

Plate and steamer from Accoutrement

LENTIL, PUMPKIN AND SPINACH CURRY

1 cup (200g) red lentils
700g pumpkin, peeled, chopped
1 tablespoon peanut oil
1 medium (150g) white
 onion, sliced
1 tablespoon grated fresh ginger
2 cloves garlic, crushed
1/4 cup (70g) mild curry paste
1 tablespoon black mustard seeds
1²/3 cups (400ml) coconut cream
350g baby spinach leaves
1 tablespoon chopped fresh
 coriander leaves

- Cook lentils in large pan of boiling water, uncovered, about 10 minutes or until tender; drain.

- Boil, steam or microwave pumpkin until tender; drain.

- Heat oil in wok; stir-fry onion, ginger and garlic until onion is browned lightly.

- Add paste and seeds; stir-fry until fragrant and hot.

- Add lentils, pumpkin and cream; stir-fry until sauce boils.

- Add spinach and coriander; stir-fry, tossing until spinach is just wilted.

SERVES 4

CHICKEN AND CORN WITH EGG ROLLS

2 eggs
1 tablespoon peanut oil
130g can creamed corn
1 tablespoon chopped fresh ginger
1 clove garlic, crushed
1 bird's-eye chilli, seeded, chopped
1 small (80g) white onion, chopped
1/2 cup (125ml) chicken stock
700g chicken thigh fillets
100g fresh baby corn
1 medium (200g) red
    capsicum, sliced
6 green onions, sliced

• Whisk eggs and 1 teaspoon of the oil in small jug.

• Brush heated wok with a little of the oil; add 1/2 of the egg mixture, swirling wok to form thin omelette. Remove omelette from wok; repeat with remaining egg mixture to make 2 omelettes.

• Roll omelettes tightly; cut each egg roll into thin slices.

• Blend or process creamed corn, ginger, garlic, chilli, white onion and stock until almost smooth.

• Cut each chicken fillet into thirds.

• Heat remaining oil in same wok; stir-fry chicken, in batches, until browned and cooked through.

• Stir-fry baby corn and capsicum in same wok until just tender.

• Return chicken to wok with creamed corn mixture; stir-fry until sauce boils.

• Add green onion and egg roll slices; stir-fry, tossing to combine ingredients.

SERVES 4

LAMB CUTLETS WITH CHINESE WATER SPINACH

12 (900g) lamb cutlets
1 teaspoon five-spice powder
1 teaspoon sugar
2 teaspoons cornflour
1/4 cup (60ml) light soy sauce
1/4 cup (60ml) black bean sauce
2 cloves garlic, crushed
2 teaspoons finely grated
    fresh ginger
2 tablespoons peanut oil
1 large (200g) brown onion, sliced
230g can water chestnuts,
    drained, chopped
400g Chinese water spinach,
    chopped coarsely

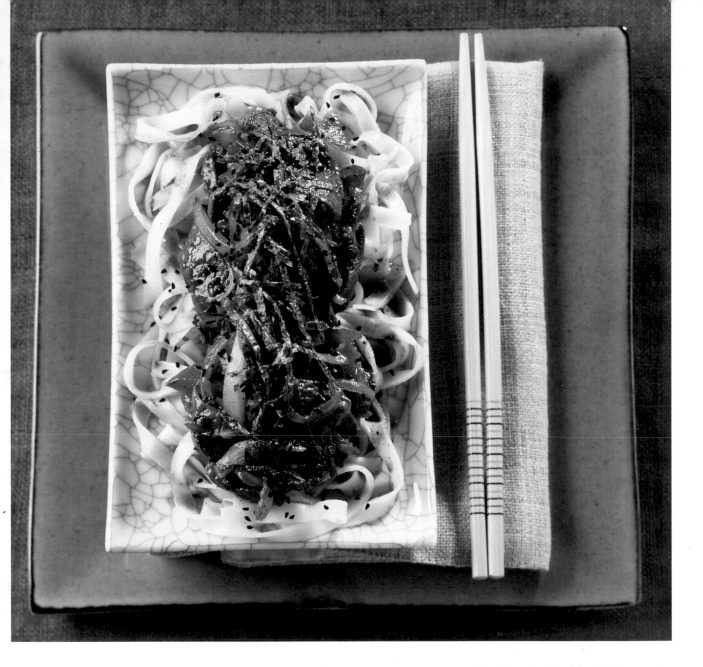

• Combine cutlets with five-spice, sugar, cornflour, 1/2 of the soy sauce, 1/2 of the black bean sauce, garlic and ginger in large bowl, cover; refrigerate 3 hours or overnight.

To cook Drain cutlets over medium bowl; reserve marinade.

• Heat 1/2 of the oil in wok; stir-fry cutlets, in batches, until browned and cooked as desired.

• Heat remaining oil in same wok; stir-fry onion and chestnuts until just tender.

• Return cutlets to wok with reserved marinade; stir-fry, tossing until sauce boils. Remove from wok; keep warm.

• Stir-fry spinach in same wok with remaining combined sauces until spinach is just wilted.

• Serve cutlets with spinach mixture.

SERVES 4

TERIYAKI BEEF WITH TOASTED NORI AND SESAME

700g beef steak, sliced thinly
1/4 cup (60ml) mirin
1/4 cup (60ml) ketjap manis
1 tablespoon rice vinegar
1 tablespoon finely chopped palm sugar
1/4 cup (60ml) fresh lime juice
2 cloves garlic, crushed
3 bird's-eye chillies, seeded, chopped finely
1 tablespoon chopped glace ginger
2 teaspoons sesame oil
375g rice stick noodles
2 tablespoons peanut oil
3 small (300g) red onions, sliced
2 tablespoons black sesame seeds
2 sheets toasted nori, shredded

• Combine beef, mirin, ketjap manis, vinegar, sugar, juice, garlic, chilli, ginger and sesame oil in large bowl, cover; refrigerate 3 hours or overnight.

To cook Place noodles in medium heat-proof bowl, cover with boiling water, stand until just tender; drain. Drain beef over medium bowl; reserve marinade.

• Heat peanut oil in wok; stir-fry beef and onion, in batches, until browned. Return beef to wok with reserved marinade; stir-fry until sauce boils.

• Add noodles, sesame seeds and nori; stir-fry, tossing to combine ingredients.

SERVES 4

Above left Chicken and corn with egg rolls
Below left Lamb cutlets with Chinese water spinach
Above Teriyaki beef with toasted nori and sesame

THAI GREEN FISH CURRY

2 tablespoons peanut oil
750g piece fresh tuna, chopped
2 medium (300g) white
  onions, chopped
2 cloves garlic, crushed
1 tablespoon finely chopped fresh
  lemon grass
1 tablespoon grated fresh ginger
2 tablespoons green curry paste
1²/₃ cups (400ml) coconut cream
2 tablespoons lime juice
1 tablespoon thick tamarind
  concentrate

1 tablespoon chopped fresh
  coriander leaves
1 cup (80g) bean sprouts
250g snow peas, sliced

• Heat ¹/₂ of the oil in wok; stir-fry fish,
in batches, until just browned.

• Heat remaining oil in same wok; stir-fry
onion, garlic, lemon grass and ginger
until onion is soft.

• Add paste; stir-fry until fragrant.

• Return fish to wok with remaining ingredients; stir-fry, tossing until sprouts are
just wilted.

SERVES 4

BEEF AND BLACK
BEAN EGG ROLLS

700g beef steak, sliced thinly
2 tablespoons soy sauce
2 cloves garlic, crushed
1 teaspoon grated fresh ginger
10 eggs
¹/₄ cup (60ml) water
¹/₂ teaspoon sesame oil
2 tablespoons peanut oil
1 large (200g) brown onion, sliced
¹/₃ cup (80ml) black bean sauce
1 medium (120g) carrot, sliced
1¹/₂ cups (120g) bean sprouts
6 green onions, sliced

• Combine beef, ¹/₂ of the soy sauce, garlic and ginger in large bowl, cover; refrigerate 3 hours or overnight.

To cook Whisk eggs, water and sesame oil in large jug.

• Brush heated wok with some of the peanut oil; add ¹/₄ cup of the egg mixture, swirling wok to form thin omelette. Remove omelette from wok; repeat with remaining egg mixture to make 8 omelettes.

• Heat remaining peanut oil in same wok; stir-fry beef mixture and brown onion, in batches, until beef is browned.

• Add remaining soy sauce and black bean sauce; cook until sauce boils.

• Add carrot to same wok; stir-fry until just tender. Add sprouts and green onion; stir-fry, tossing to combine vegetables.

• Divide beef mixture among omelettes; roll to enclose filling. Cut egg rolls in half; serve with vegetables.

SERVES 4

GARLIC BEEF AND VERMICELLI

500g beef steak, sliced thinly
4 cloves garlic, crushed
¹/₂ cup (125ml) oyster sauce
4 small dried red chillies
250g rice vermicelli
2 tablespoons peanut oil
200g fresh baby corn, sliced
400g broccoli, cut into florets
**2 medium (200g) red
    capsicums, sliced**
2 tablespoons brown sugar
2 tablespoons light soy sauce

• Combine beef, garlic, ¹/₂ of the oyster sauce and chillies in medium bowl, cover; refrigerate 3 hours or overnight.

To cook Place vermicelli in large heatproof bowl, cover with boiling water, stand until just tender; drain.

• Heat oil in wok; stir-fry beef mixture, in batches, until browned.

• Stir-fry corn, broccoli and capsicum in same wok until just tender.

• Return beef mixture to wok with remaining oyster sauce, sugar and soy sauce; stir-fry until sauce boils.

• Add vermicelli; stir-fry, tossing to combine ingredients.

SERVES 4

Left Thai green fish curry
Above right Beef and black bean egg rolls
Right Garlic beef and vermicelli

AROMATIC CHICKEN WITH THAI EGGPLANT

2 cups coarsely chopped fresh
   coriander leaves
2 tablespoons finely chopped fresh
   lemon grass
1 tablespoon finely grated lime rind
2 tablespoons lime juice
2 tablespoons grated fresh ginger
1 tablespoon ground turmeric
1 tablespoon ground coriander
1 tablespoon ground cumin
1/3 cup (80ml) peanut oil
700g single chicken breast fillets,
   sliced thinly
250g Thai eggplants
1 medium (150g) brown
   onion, sliced
3 cups (240g) bean sprouts

• Blend or process coriander leaves,
lemon grass, rind, juice, ginger, turmeric,
ground coriander and cumin with 1/2 of
the oil until mixture forms a paste.

• Combine chicken in large bowl with
coriander paste, mix well, cover;
refrigerate 3 hours or overnight.

To cook Discard stems from eggplants;
stir-fry eggplants in dry heated wok for
2 minutes, remove from wok.

• Heat remaining oil in same wok; stir-fry
chicken mixture and onion, in batches,
until chicken is cooked through.

• Return chicken mixture to wok with
eggplants and sprouts; stir-fry, tossing
until sprouts are just wilted.

SERVES 4

HOT-SOUR CHICKEN AND SNAKE BEANS

4 cloves garlic, crushed
2 tablespoons Lemon
   Pepper Seasoning
4 bird's-eye chillies, seeded,
   chopped finely
1/2 cup (125ml) water
2 tablespoons thick tamarind
   concentrate
1kg single chicken breast fillets,
   sliced thinly
350g snake beans, chopped
1 tablespoon peanut oil
2 large (600g) red onions, sliced
1 tablespoon sugar
1/4 cup (60ml) chicken stock

• Combine garlic, Seasoning, chilli, water, tamarind and chicken in medium bowl, cover; refrigerate 3 hours or overnight.

To cook Boil, steam or microwave beans until just tender; drain.

• Heat oil in wok; stir-fry chicken mixture and onion, in batches, until chicken is browned and cooked through.

• Return chicken mixture to wok with beans, sugar and stock; stir-fry, tossing until sauce boils.

• Serve chicken mixture with pappadums, if desired.

SERVES 6

SICHUAN BEEF WITH KAFFIR LIME LEAVES

1kg beef steak, sliced thinly
1 tablespoon Lemon
   Pepper Seasoning
2 tablespoons Sichuan
   peppercorns, crushed
2 tablespoons grated fresh ginger
8 kaffir lime leaves, shredded
1/3 cup finely chopped fresh
   coriander root
1/3 cup (80ml) peanut oil
350g rice stick noodles
2 small (200g) red onions, sliced
3 cloves garlic, crushed
1/4 cup (60ml) lime juice
1/4 cup (60ml) sweet chilli sauce
200g broccoli, chopped
200g tat soi, chopped
250g Chinese water spinach, chopped
1 cup fresh coriander leaves

• Combine beef, Seasoning, pepper, ginger, lime leaves, coriander root and 1/2 of the oil in medium bowl, cover; refrigerate 3 hours or overnight.

To cook Place noodles in medium heat-proof bowl, cover with boiling water, stand until just tender; drain.

• Heat remaining oil in wok; stir-fry beef mixture, onion and garlic, in batches, until beef is browned.

• Add juice and sauce to same wok; cook over heat until mixture boils. Remove from wok. Stir-fry broccoli in same wok until just tender.

• Return beef mixture to wok with tat soi, spinach, coriander leaves and sauce; stir-fry, tossing until sauce boils.

• Serve beef mixture with noodles.

SERVES 4 TO 6

Above left Aromatic chicken with Thai eggplant
Below left Hot-sour chicken and snake beans
Right Sichuan beef with kaffir lime leaves

WARM THAI BEEF SALAD

700g beef steak, sliced thinly
1 tablespoon grated fresh ginger
1 tablespoon finely grated lime rind
1 tablespoon lime juice
**4 bird's-eye chillies, seeded,
  chopped finely**
**2 tablespoons finely chopped fresh
  lemon grass**
**1/4 cup coarsely chopped fresh
  coriander leaves**
250g rice vermicelli
2 tablespoons peanut oil
**1 medium (150g) brown
  onion, sliced**
**1 medium ((200g) red
  capsicum, chopped**
**1 medium (170g) cucumber,
  seeded, chopped**
4 green onions, sliced

LEMON MINT DRESSING
1/2 cup (125ml) peanut oil
1/3 cup (60ml) lemon juice
1/4 cup chopped fresh mint leaves
2 cloves garlic, crushed
2 teaspoons sugar

• Combine beef, ginger, rind, juice, chilli,
lemon grass and 1/2 of the coriander in
large bowl, cover; refrigerate 3 hours or
overnight.

To cook Place vermicelli in medium
heatproof bowl, cover with boiling water,
stand until just tender; drain.

• Heat oil in wok; stir-fry beef mixture and
brown onion, in batches, until beef is
browned and cooked as desired.

• Gently toss vermicelli and beef mixture
in large bowl with capsicum, cucumber,
green onion, remaining coriander and
Lemon Mint Dressing.

Lemon Mint Dressing Combine all
ingredients in jar; shake well.
SERVES 4

HOKKIEN PEANUT BEEF

700g beef steak, sliced thinly
**1 cup (150g) roasted peanuts,
  chopped coarsely**
2 tablespoons soy sauce
1 tablespoon grated fresh ginger
1 tablespoon finely grated lime rind
1 tablespoon lime juice
450g Hokkien noodles
2 tablespoons peanut oil
500g baby bok choy, halved
200g baby tat soi leaves

• Combine beef with 1/2 of the peanuts,
sauce, ginger, rind and juice in large bowl,
cover; refrigerate 3 hours or overnight.

To cook Rinse noodles under hot water; drain. Transfer noodles to large bowl; separate with fork.

• Heat oil in wok; stir-fry beef mixture, in batches, until browned.

• Return beef to wok with bok choy, tat soi and noodles; stir-fry, tossing until bok choy and tat soi are just wilted.

• Serve beef and noodles sprinkled with remaining peanuts.

SERVES 4

CANTONESE SPINACH AND ALMONDS

2 teaspoons peanut oil
1/3 cup (25g) flaked almonds
2 tablespoons sweet sherry
2 tablespoons soy sauce
2 tablespoons honey
1 clove garlic, crushed
1/2 teaspoon sesame oil
1kg spinach, trimmed
6 green onions, chopped

• Heat peanut oil in wok; stir-fry nuts until just browned, remove from wok.

• Cook sherry, soy sauce, honey, garlic and oil in same wok until sauce boils.

• Add spinach and onion; stir-fry, tossing until spinach is just wilted.

• Serve spinach mixture with nuts sprinkled over the top.

SERVES 4

Above left Warm Thai beef salad
Below left Hokkien peanut beef
Below Cantonese spinach and almonds

COCONUT CURRIED VEGETABLES

1 medium (400g) kumara, sliced
1 small (1kg) cauliflower, chopped
2 tablespoons ghee
2 teaspoons ground cumin
1 teaspoon ground coriander
1 teaspoon garam masala
2 teaspoons ground turmeric
$1/2$ teaspoon sweet paprika
1 large (200g) brown onion, sliced
2 cloves garlic, crushed
2 medium (240g) carrots, sliced
400g broccoli, chopped
350g snake beans, chopped
$1^2/3$ cups (400ml) coconut cream

BARBECUED PORK WITH PEANUTS AND NOODLES

Ready-to-eat barbecued pork can be purchased from specialty Asian food stores.

200g fresh rice noodles
200g snow peas
1 tablespoon peanut oil
1 medium (150g) brown onion, sliced
1 small (150g) red capsicum, sliced
2 tablespoons finely chopped palm sugar
2 tablespoons soy sauce
600g barbecued pork, sliced thinly
1 cup (150g) roasted peanuts, chopped coarsely
2$1/2$ cups (200g) bean sprouts
200g baby tat soi

• Place noodles in medium heatproof bowl, cover with boiling water, stand until just tender; drain.

• Cut snow peas lengthways thinly.

• Heat oil in wok; stir-fry onion, capsicum and sugar until onion is browned.

• Add snow peas, noodles and remaining ingredients to wok; stir-fry, tossing until sprouts and tat soi are just wilted.

SERVES 4

- Boil, steam or microwave kumara and cauliflower until just tender; drain.

- Heat ghee in wok; stir-fry spices until fragrant. Add onion and garlic; stir-fry until onion is browned lightly.

- Add carrot, broccoli and beans; stir-fry until vegetables are just tender.

- Add kumara, cauliflower and cream; stir-fry, tossing until sauce boils.

SERVES 4 TO 6

Left Barbecued pork with peanuts and noodles
Below Coconut curried vegetables
Right Three-flavours chicken wings

THREE-FLAVOURS CHICKEN WINGS

1.5kg chicken wings
2 tablespoons peanut oil
2 cloves garlic, crushed
1 tablespoon grated fresh ginger
1 medium (400g) corn cob, sliced
1 medium (120g) carrot, chopped
1 medium (350g) leek, chopped
1 medium (200g) red capsicum, chopped
1/4 cup (60ml) oyster sauce
2 tablespoons hoisin sauce
2 tablespoons plum sauce
2 tablespoons chopped fresh coriander leaves

- Remove and discard tip from each chicken wing; cut wings in half at joint.

- Cook chicken in large pan of boiling water, uncovered, about 5 minutes or until almost cooked through; drain.

- Heat 1/2 of the oil in wok; stir-fry chicken, garlic and ginger, in batches, until chicken is cooked through.

- Heat remaining oil in same wok; stir-fry corn, carrot, leek and capsicum until vegetables are just tender.

- Return chicken mixture to wok with combined sauces; stir-fry, tossing until sauce boils.

- Serve chicken mixture sprinkled with coriander leaves.

SERVES 6

CHENGDU-STYLE DUCK

**1 tablespoon finely chopped fresh
  lemon grass**
**1 tablespoon coarsely chopped fresh
  mint leaves**
2 cloves garlic, crushed
2 teaspoons Sichuan peppercorns
**2 teaspoons finely grated
  lemon rind**
1/2 teaspoon hot paprika
**600g duck breast fillets,
  sliced thinly**
2 tablespoons cornflour
1 tablespoon peanut oil
400g baby bok choy, sliced
1¹/2 cups (120g) bean sprouts
1/4 cup (60ml) sweet chilli sauce

• Using blender or mortar and pestle,
make a paste of lemon grass, mint, garlic,
peppercorns, rind and paprika.

• Combine duck in large bowl with spice
paste, cornflour and oil, mix well, cover;
refrigerate 3 hours or overnight.

To cook Stir-fry duck mixture in heated
wok, in batches, until browned and
cooked through.

• Drain all but 1 tablespoon of fat from
wok. Stir-fry bok choy and sprouts until
just wilted.

• Return duck mixture to wok with sauce;
stir-fry, tossing to combine ingredients.

SERVES 4

PRAWNS WITH LEMON GRASS AND MINT

750g medium uncooked prawns
**2 tablespoons chopped fresh
  mint leaves**
**2 tablespoons finely chopped fresh
  lemon grass**
2 cloves garlic, crushed
1 teaspoon finely grated lemon rind
2 tablespoons lemon juice
2 teaspoons sambal oelek
1 medium (120g) carrot
1/4 cup (60ml) peanut oil
100g snow peas, sliced
1 tablespoon brown vinegar
1 teaspoon brown sugar
1 teaspoon soy sauce

• Shell and devein prawns, leaving tails intact. Combine prawns in large bowl with mint, lemon grass, garlic, rind, juice and sambal, cover; refrigerate 3 hours or overnight.

To cook Heat 1 tablespoon of the oil in wok; stir-fry prawn mixture, in batches, until prawns are changed in colour.

• Using vegetable peeler, slice carrot into thin ribbons. Add snow peas and carrot strips to same wok; stir-fry, tossing until just tender.

• Return prawn mixture to wok; stir-fry, tossing with vegetables. To serve, drizzle combined remaining oil, vinegar, sugar and soy sauce over prawn mixture.

SERVES 4

THREE-TREASURE MUSHROOMS AND PORK

700g pork fillets, sliced thinly
1/4 cup (60ml) soy sauce
1/4 cup (60ml) oyster sauce
2 tablespoons Chinese rice wine
1 tablespoon honey
1 tablespoon brown sugar
1 clove garlic, crushed
1/2 teaspoon ground cinnamon
6 dried shiitake mushrooms
2 tablespoons peanut oil
150g oyster mushrooms
200g Swiss brown
**   mushrooms, halved**

• Combine pork, soy sauce, 1 tablespoon of the oyster sauce, wine, honey, sugar, garlic and cinnamon in medium bowl, cover; refrigerate 3 hours or overnight.

To cook Place dried mushrooms in small heatproof bowl, cover with boiling water; stand 20 minutes. Drain mushrooms over small bowl, reserve liquid. Discard stems; cut caps in half.

• Heat 1/2 of the oil in wok; stir-fry pork mixture and dried mushroom pieces, in batches, until pork is browned and cooked as desired.

• Heat remaining oil in same wok; stir-fry oyster and Swiss brown mushrooms until just soft.

• Return pork mixture to wok with reserved liquid and remaining oyster sauce; stir-fry, tossing until sauce boils.

SERVES 4

Left Chengdu-style duck
Above right Prawns with lemon grass and mint
Right Three-treasure mushrooms and pork

East meets West

Cooking that happily married ingredients and flavours of the Orient with those of Europe first emerged in the '70s and has since become universally known as fusion food or crossover cuisine. But no matter what it's called, it's the food we all eat today, and these two dishes are perfect examples – light, imaginative and quick. Their recipes appear later in this chapter but you can see the delightful surprise when two cultures meet on a single plate. Pistachios merge with tofu in one recipe, while aromatic lashings of lemon grass and coriander enliven the more subtle appeal of chicken and asparagus in another... sometimes a picture can be worth more than a thousand words.

MANGO CHICKEN WITH SPINACH AND KUMARA

1/4 cup (60ml) peanut oil
500g kumara, sliced
750g minced chicken
1 medium (150g) white
  onion, chopped
1 clove garlic, crushed
1 tablespoon ground cumin
1/3 cup (90g) mango chutney
2 tablespoons lime juice
150g snow peas, halved
250g spinach, trimmed, chopped

• Heat 1/2 of the oil in wok; stir-fry kumara, in batches, until just tender.

• Heat remaining oil in wok; stir-fry chicken with onion, garlic and cumin, in batches, until chicken is browned and cooked through.

• Return chicken mixture and kumara to wok with remaining ingredients; stir-fry, tossing, until spinach is just wilted.

SERVES 4

HUNGARIAN-STYLE PAPRIKA PORK

1kg pork fillets, sliced thinly
1/4 cup (25g) sweet paprika
5 cloves garlic, crushed
1 cup (250ml) chicken stock
12 star-anise
2 tablespoons finely grated
  lemon rind
300g fresh thin egg noodles
1 tablespoon peanut oil
2 medium (340g) red onions, sliced
1 teaspoon sugar

• Combine pork with paprika and garlic in large bowl, cover; refrigerate 3 hours or overnight.

To cook Combine stock, star-anise and rind in small pan, bring to boil; simmer, uncovered, until reduced by half. Strain liquid into small heatproof bowl; discard star-anise and rind.

• Meanwhile, cook noodles in large pan of boiling water, uncovered, until just tender; drain. Cover to keep warm.

• Heat oil in wok; stir-fry pork mixture with the onion, in batches, until pork is browned.

• Return pork mixture to wok, add sugar and reserved liquid; stir-fry, tossing until sauce boils.

• Serve pork on noodles.

SERVES 6

Left Mango chicken with spinach and kumara
Right Hungarian-style paprika pork

LIME AND LEMON GRASS CHILLI OCTOPUS

2kg baby octopus, halved
1/2 cup (125ml) olive oil
1/4 cup (60ml) dry red wine
1/4 cup finely chopped fresh lemon grass
2 tablespoons finely grated lime rind
1 tablespoon finely grated lemon rind
3 cloves garlic, crushed
4 bird's-eye chillies, seeded, chopped finely
2 teaspoons grated fresh ginger
1 cup (250ml) peanut oil

16 wonton wrappers
1 tablespoon sea salt
2 teaspoons chilli powder
1 medium (350g) leek
1 tablespoon sweet chilli sauce

• Combine octopus, olive oil, wine, lemon grass, rinds, garlic, fresh chilli and ginger in large bowl, cover; refrigerate 3 hours or overnight.

To cook Drain octopus over medium bowl; reserve 1/2 cup of the marinade.

• Heat peanut oil in wok; stir-fry wonton wrappers, in batches, until browned lightly. Drain wrappers on absorbent paper; while still warm, sprinkle wrappers with combined salt and chilli powder.

• Halve leek lengthways; cut halves into long thin strips.

• Reheat peanut oil in wok; deep-fry leek, in batches, until browned lightly. Drain on absorbent paper.

• Drain peanut oil from wok; stir-fry octopus, in batches, until tender.

• Return octopus to wok with reserved marinade and chilli sauce; stir-fry, tossing until sauce boils.

• Serve octopus, topped with leek, with chilli wrappers.

SERVES 4 TO 6

TANDOORI BEEF, SUGARED ALMONDS AND BANANAS

700g beef steak, sliced thinly
1/2 cup (130ml) tandoori paste
2 teaspoons ground cumin
2 teaspoons ground coriander
1/3 cup (60ml) water
1/4 cup fresh curry leaves, torn
50g butter
1/3 cup (75g) firmly packed
   brown sugar
1/4 cup (65g) finely chopped
   palm sugar
1 cup (160g) blanched
   whole almonds
2 small (260g) bananas, sliced

2 tablespoons peanut oil
3 small (300g) red onions, sliced
3 cloves garlic, crushed
1 tablespoon grated fresh ginger

• Combine beef, paste, cumin, coriander, the water and curry leaves in large bowl, cover; refrigerate 3 hours or overnight.

To cook Heat 1/2 of the butter, 1/2 of the brown sugar and all of the palm sugar in wok, add nuts; cook, stirring constantly, 2 minutes. Place nuts on greaseproof paper in single layer; cool. Wipe wok clean with absorbent paper.

• Heat remaining butter and remaining brown sugar in same wok, add banana slices; cook, turning gently, until banana softens and is caramelised lightly. Place

banana mixture on greaseproof paper in single layer; wipe wok clean.

• Heat oil in same wok; stir-fry beef mixture, onion, garlic and ginger, in batches, until browned.

• Serve beef with almonds and banana.

SERVES 4

Left Lime and lemon grass chilli octopus
Below Tandoori beef, sugared almonds and bananas

HOT AND SWEET CHICKEN WINGS WITH KUMARA

1kg chicken wings
1 medium (400g) kumara
2 tablespoons olive oil
2 medium (300g) brown
**   onions, sliced**
2 cloves garlic, crushed
1/4 cup (60ml) barbecue sauce
1/4 cup (60ml) tomato sauce
2 tablespoons honey
2 teaspoons sambal oelek

• Remove and discard tip from each chicken wing; cut wings in half at joint.

• Cook chicken in large pan of boiling water, uncovered, about 5 minutes or until almost cooked through; drain.

• Cut kumara into matchstick-size pieces.

• Heat 1/2 of the oil in wok; stir-fry chicken, in batches, until browned.

• Heat remaining oil in same wok; stir-fry kumara, onion and garlic, in batches, until kumara is just tender.

• Return chicken and kumara mixture to wok with combined sauces, honey and sambal; stir-fry, tossing until sauce boils.

SERVES 4

TAMARIND LAMB WITH SAFFRON BREADCRUMBS

3 cloves garlic, crushed
1 tablespoon thick tamarind
**   concentrate**
6 kaffir lime leaves, torn
2 tablespoons finely chopped
**   fresh lemon grass**
2 tablespoons brown sugar
1kg lamb fillets, sliced thinly
1 tablespoon peanut oil
2 large (400g) brown onions, sliced
80g butter
1/2 teaspoon saffron threads
2 cups (140g) stale white
**   breadcrumbs**
2 tablespoons chopped fresh chives
1/2 cup (125ml) beef stock

• Combine garlic, tamarind, lime leaves, lemon grass and sugar with lamb in large bowl, cover; refrigerate 3 hours or overnight.

To cook Heat oil in wok; stir-fry lamb mixture and onion, in batches, until lamb is browned. Wipe the wok clean with absorbent paper.

• Heat butter in same wok; stir-fry saffron until just fragrant. Add breadcrumbs and chives; cook, tossing until breadcrumbs are browned and crisp. Remove breadcrumb mixture from wok.

- Return lamb mixture to wok with stock; stir-fry, tossing until sauce boils.

- Add ¹/₂ of the saffron breadcrumbs to wok; stir-fry, tossing to combine with other ingredients.

- Serve lamb sprinkled with remaining saffron breadcrumbs.

SERVES 6

LEMON-GRASS CHICKEN

700g single chicken breast fillets, sliced thickly
¹/₄ cup finely chopped fresh lemon grass
1 tablespoon grated fresh ginger
4 kaffir lime leaves, shredded
4 baby (240g) eggplants
coarse cooking salt
500g asparagus
¹/₄ cup (60ml) peanut oil
1 medium (150g) white onion, sliced
2 teaspoons ground cumin
1 tablespoon finely grated lemon rind
1 tablespoon lemon juice

- Combine chicken, lemon grass, ginger and lime leaves in large bowl, cover; refrigerate 3 hours or overnight.

To cook Halve eggplants lengthways; cut halves into 2cm pieces. Place eggplant in colander, sprinkle all over with salt; stand 30 minutes. Rinse eggplant under cold water; pat dry with absorbent paper.

- Cut asparagus into 5cm lengths.

- Heat 1 tablespoon of the oil in wok; stir-fry chicken mixture and onion, in batches, until chicken is browned and cooked through.

- Heat remaining oil in wok; stir-fry eggplant with cumin until tender.

- Return chicken mixture to wok, add asparagus, rind and juice; stir-fry, tossing to combine with eggplant mixture.

- Serve chicken with fresh rice noodles tossed with poppy seeds, if desired.

SERVES 4

Left Hot and sweet chicken wings with kumara
Above right Tamarind lamb with saffron breadcrumbs
Right Lemon-grass chicken

SCALLOPS WITH NOODLES IN SWEET BUTTER SAUCE

600g large white scallops
    (approximately 24)
1/2 cup (125ml) fish stock
1/4 cup (60ml) coconut cream
1 teaspoon ground cinnamon
450g thin fresh egg noodles
2 tablespoons peanut oil
100g butter
1 tablespoon finely chopped
    palm sugar
3 kaffir lime leaves, shredded
1/4 cup (60ml) ketjup manis
1/2 cup (60g) roasted
    hazelnuts, chopped

• Combine scallops, 1/2 of the stock, cream and cinnamon in large bowl, cover; refrigerate 3 hours or overnight.

To cook Drain scallops over medium bowl; reserve 1/4 cup of the marinade.

• Place noodles in large heatproof bowl, cover with boiling water, stand until just tender; drain. Cover to keep warm.

• Heat oil in wok; stir-fry scallop mixture, in batches, until just tender. Cover to keep warm.

• Melt butter in same wok; stir-fry sugar, lime leaves, ketjup, remaining stock and reserved marinade until sauce boils.

• Serve scallops and noodles drizzled with butter sauce and sprinkled with nuts.

SERVES 4

CHILLI, ROCKET AND LAMB NOODLE SALAD

Anaheim chillies are fresh green chillies averaging 10cm in length and having a rich but not fiery-hot flavour. It is the chilli used in that Mexican favourite chiles rellenos, and is available here from specialty greengrocers if you order it in advance.

1 medium (150g) brown
    onion, chopped
2 cloves garlic, chopped
2 bird's-eye chillies, seeded,
    chopped finely
2 teaspoons ground cumin
2 teaspoons ground coriander
1/4 cup (60ml) olive oil
1/3 cup (80ml) lime juice
1/2 teaspoon sugar
700g lamb fillets, sliced thinly
120g rice vermicelli
1/3 cup firmly packed fresh
    basil leaves
6 anaheim chillies, sliced
150g baby rocket leaves

• Blend or process onion, garlic, bird's-eye chilli, cumin, coriander, 1 tablespoon of the oil, juice and sugar until smooth.

• Combine lamb with pureed spice mixture in large bowl, cover; refrigerate 3 hours or overnight.

To cook Place noodles in medium heatproof bowl, cover with boiling water, stand until just tender; drain. Chop with scissors into 10cm lengths.

• Heat remaining oil in wok; stir-fry lamb mixture, in batches, until browned.

• Add noodles, basil, anaheim chilli and rocket to wok with lamb; stir-fry, tossing until ingredients are combined.

SERVES 4

Left Scallops with noodles in sweet butter sauce
Above Chilli, rocket and lamb noodle salad

LAMB PAPRIKASH WITH BROWN LENTILS

1 tablespoon finely grated lime rind
1 tablespoon sweet paprika
2 teaspoons ground cumin
2 teaspoons ground cardamom
2 teaspoons ground ginger
1/4 cup (60ml) peanut oil
1kg lamb eye of loin, sliced thinly
1 cup (200g) brown lentils
1/3 cup (80ml) dry red wine
1 litre (4 cups) beef stock
1/2 cup (125ml) peanut oil, extra

4 pappadums
3 cloves garlic, crushed
2 medium (340g) red onions, sliced
4 bird's-eye chillies, seeded,
  chopped finely
1/4 cup (60ml) beef stock, extra
1/4 cup (60ml) lime juice

• Combine rind, paprika, cumin, cardamom, ginger, oil and lamb in large bowl, cover; refrigerate 3 hours or overnight.

To cook Combine lentils, wine and stock in medium pan, bring to boil; simmer, covered, about 30 minutes or until lentils are just tender.

• Heat extra oil in wok; fry pappadums until crisp. Drain on absorbent paper; break into large pieces. Discard cooled oil; wipe wok clean with absorbent paper.

• Stir-fry lamb mixture in same wok with garlic, onion and chilli, in batches, until lamb is browned.

• Return lamb mixture to wok with lentils, extra stock and juice; stir-fry, tossing until sauce boils.

• Serve lamb and lentils topped with pappadum pieces.

SERVES 6

BEEF WITH PISTACHIOS AND BEETROOT PUREE

1kg beef steak, sliced thinly
3 cloves garlic, crushed
4 bird's-eye chillies, seeded,
  chopped finely
2 tablespoons balsamic vinegar
1/4 cup (60ml) peanut oil
1/4 cup (60ml) orange juice
1 large (200g) beetroot, quartered
4 kaffir lime leaves
1 tablespoon sugar
1/4 cup (60ml) water
1 cup (250ml) orange juice, extra
1 tablespoon peanut oil, extra
3 small (300g) red onions, sliced
1/2 cup (75g) pistachios, toasted

• Combine beef, garlic, chilli, vinegar, oil and juice in large bowl, cover; refrigerate 3 hours or overnight.

To cook Combine beetroot, lime leaves, sugar, the water and extra juice in small pan; bring to boil. Simmer, covered, about 20 minutes or until beetroot is tender. Discard lime leaves; blend or process beetroot mixture until pureed. Place beetroot puree in small bowl; cover to keep warm.

• Heat extra oil in wok; stir-fry beef mixture and onion, in batches, until browned.

• Serve beef with beetroot puree and nuts.

SERVES 4

Left Lamb paprikash with brown lentils
Right Beef with pistachios and beetroot puree

PEANUT-CRUSTED LEMON GRASS CHICKEN

700g single chicken breast fillets, sliced thinly
4 bird's-eye chillies, seeded, chopped finely
2 tablespoons grated fresh ginger
4 cloves garlic, crushed
6 kaffir lime leaves, chopped
400g sugar snap peas
1/4 cup (60ml) peanut oil
2 medium (340g) red onions, sliced
1 cup (150g) plain flour, approximately
2 eggs, beaten lightly
2 cups (300g) raw peanuts, chopped finely
1/2 cup finely chopped fresh lemon grass
1/4 cup (60ml) chicken stock
2 tablespoons sweet chilli sauce

• Combine chicken, chilli, ginger, garlic and lime leaves in large bowl, cover; refrigerate 3 hours or overnight.

To cook Boil, steam or microwave peas until just tender; drain.

• Heat 1 tablespoon of the oil in wok; stir-fry onion, in batches, until just browned.

• Dip chicken in flour; shake away excess. Dip chicken in egg then, using hand, press on combined nuts and lemon grass.

• Heat remaining oil in same wok; stir-fry chicken, in batches, until browned and cooked through. Drain chicken on absorbent paper; cover to keep warm. Wipe wok clean with absorbent paper.

• Return onion to wok with combined stock and sauce; stir-fry until sauce boils, add peas.

• Serve onion mixture with chicken.
SERVES 6

TURKISH LAMB WITH SPINACH AND PINE NUTS

1 tablespoon olive oil
1/2 cup (80g) pine nuts
750g minced lamb
2 large (400g) brown onions, chopped
2 cloves garlic, crushed
4 bird's-eye chillies, seeded, chopped finely
1 tablespoon ground coriander
1 tablespoon ground cumin
500g spinach, trimmed, chopped
1/4 cup chopped fresh mint leaves
4 large pitta breads
300ml yogurt
1 tablespoon lemon juice

• Heat 1/2 of the oil in wok; stir-fry pine nuts until just browned lightly. Drain on absorbent paper.

• Stir-fry lamb in same wok, in batches, until browned.

• Heat remaining oil in same wok; stir-fry onion, garlic, chilli, coriander and cumin until onion is browned lightly.

• Return lamb to wok with nuts, spinach and mint; stir-fry, tossing until spinach is just wilted.

• Divide lamb among pitta; serve with combined yogurt and juice.
SERVES 4

Left Peanut-crusted lemon grass chicken
Above Turkish lamb with spinach and pine nuts

PESTO BEEF SALAD

We used a traditional basil-flavoured prepared pesto in this recipe.

700g beef steak, sliced thinly
1/3 cup (90g) pesto
1 clove garlic, crushed
1 tablespoon olive oil
1 medium (170g) red onion, sliced
1 medium (200g) red capsicum, sliced
1 medium (200g) green capsicum, sliced
350g watercress
250g cherry tomatoes, quartered
2 tablespoons pesto, extra
2 tablespoons olive oil, extra
1/4 cup (60ml) lemon juice
1 teaspoon sugar
3 bird's-eye chillies, seeded, chopped finely

• Combine beef with the pesto and garlic in large bowl, cover; refrigerate 3 hours or overnight.

To cook Heat oil in wok; stir-fry beef mixture and onion, in batches, until beef is browned.

• Stir-fry capsicums in wok until tender; combine with beef mixture in large bowl.

• Place watercress and tomato in bowl; toss with combined extra pesto, extra oil, juice, sugar and chilli.

SERVES 4

LAMB, DEEP-FRIED NOODLES AND EGGPLANT MASH

700g lamb eye of loin, sliced thinly
1 clove garlic, crushed
1/4 cup (60g) olive paste
1 tablespoon lemon juice
2 medium (600g) eggplants
coarse cooking salt
2 tablespoons olive oil
1 clove garlic, crushed, extra
1/4 teaspoon ground nutmeg
2 tablespoons yogurt
2 tablespoons tahini
vegetable oil, for deep-frying
100g bean thread noodles

• Combine lamb, garlic, paste and juice in large bowl, cover; refrigerate 3 hours or overnight.

To cook Slice eggplants thickly; sprinkle slices on both sides with salt; stand 20 minutes. Rinse eggplant under cold water; pat dry with absorbent paper.

• Heat 1/2 of the olive oil in wok; stir-fry eggplant, in batches, until soft. Drain eggplant on absorbent paper; wipe wok clean with absorbent paper.

- Blend or process eggplant with extra garlic, nutmeg, yogurt and tahini until almost smooth.

- Drain lamb; discard marinade. Heat remaining olive oil in same wok; stir-fry lamb, in batches, until browned.

- Heat vegetable oil in medium pan; deep-fry noodles, in batches, until puffed. Drain on absorbent paper.

- Serve noodles topped with eggplant mash and lamb.

SERVES 4

CITRUS COCONUT FISH BALLS

**700g firm white fish fillets,
    chopped coarsely**
**1 medium (150g) white
    onion, chopped**
3 bird's-eye chillies, seeded, sliced
**1 tablespoon chopped fresh
    basil leaves**
1 clove garlic, crushed
1 egg
vegetable oil, for deep-frying
1 tablespoon peanut oil
**1 medium (150g) white onion,
    chopped, extra**
**2 bird's-eye chillies, seeded, sliced
    finely, extra**
**1 tablespoon finely chopped
    fresh lemon grass**
300g snow peas
**2 tablespoons finely sliced
    lime rind**
1 2/3 cups (400ml) coconut milk
1/4 cup (60ml) lime juice
150g snow pea sprouts

- Blend or process fish, onion, chilli, basil, garlic and egg until mixture forms a paste. Using hands, shape level tablespoons of mixture into balls, cover; refrigerate 3 hours or overnight.

To cook Heat vegetable oil in wok; deep-fry fish balls until browned and cooked through. Drain fish balls on absorbent paper. Discard cooled oil; wipe wok clean with absorbent paper.

- Heat peanut oil in wok; stir-fry extra onion, extra chilli and lemon grass until onion is browned lightly.

- Stir-fry snow peas, rind and milk until sauce boils. Add fish balls; stir-fry, tossing to coat in sauce.

- Just before serving, toss juice and sprouts through fish ball mixture.

SERVES 4

Left Pesto beef salad
Above right Lamb, deep-fried noodles and eggplant mash
Right Citrus coconut fish balls

BUTTERFLIED SALT AND PEPPER PRAWNS

3 teaspoons sea salt
3 teaspoons cracked black pepper
1/4 cup (25g) Lemon Pepper
   Seasoning
2 tablespoons finely grated
   lemon rind
2 tablespoons finely grated
   lime rind
2 tablespoons dried onion flakes
1.5kg large uncooked prawns
1/4 cup (60ml) peanut oil
4 green onions, sliced
2 cloves garlic, crushed
2 bird's-eye chillies, seeded,
   chopped finely
1/4 cup (60ml) fish stock
2 tablespoons sweet chilli sauce

• Combine salt, pepper, Seasoning, rinds and onion flakes in small bowl.

• Shell and devein prawns, leaving tails intact. Slice halfway through each prawn from the back; press prawns firmly into salt mixture to coat both sides. Place prawns on tray, cover; refrigerate 3 hours or overnight.

To cook Heat 2 tablespoons of the oil in wok; stir-fry prawns, in batches, until prawns are just changed in colour.

• Heat remaining oil in same wok; stir-fry onion, garlic and chilli until vegetables soften slightly.

• Add combined stock and sauce; stir-fry, tossing until mixture boils.

• Serve prawns with stir-fried green vegetable such as choy sum, if desired.

SERVES 4

PORK WITH CHILLI PLUM SAUCE

4 medium (450g) plums,
   seeded, sliced
1/4 cup (60ml) lime juice
4 bird's-eye chillies, seeded,
   chopped finely
3 cloves garlic, crushed
1kg pork fillets, sliced thinly
2 tablespoons peanut oil
2 medium (300g) white
   onions, sliced
3 large (270g) egg tomatoes, sliced
1/2 cup (125ml) plum sauce
1/4 cup (60ml) chicken stock

LEMON-MYRTLE CHILLI BEEF

If you cannot find the bottled sweet lemon myrtle and chilli sauce called for in this recipe, substitute a mixture of 1 tablespoon grated lemon rind, 1/4 cup (60ml) lemon juice and 1/2 cup (125ml) sweet chilli sauce.

700g beef steak, sliced thinly
3/4 cup (180ml) sweet lemon myrtle and chilli sauce
2 cloves garlic, crushed
1 tablespoon vegetable oil
200g snow peas, chopped
500g silverbeet, trimmed, shredded
2 tablespoons chopped fresh coriander leaves

• Combine beef, 1/2 cup of the sauce and garlic in large bowl, cover; refrigerate 3 hours or overnight.

To cook Heat oil in wok; stir-fry beef mixture, in batches, until browned.

• Return the beef mixture to wok, add snow peas, silverbeet and remaining sauce; stir-fry, tossing until silverbeet is just wilted.

• Serve beef mixture sprinkled with coriander leaves.

SERVES 4

Far left Butterflied salt and pepper prawns
Left Pork with chilli plum sauce
Below Lemon-myrtle chilli beef

White serving bowl from Orson & Blake Collectables

• Blend or process 1/2 of the plum slices with juice, chilli and garlic until mixture forms a paste. Combine plum mixture with pork in large bowl, cover; refrigerate 3 hours or overnight.

To cook Heat oil in wok; stir-fry the pork mixture and onion, in batches, until browned.

• Return pork mixture to wok, add remaining plum, tomato, sauce and stock; stir-fry, tossing until sauce boils.

SERVES 6

Bowl and chopsticks from Made in Japan

SESAME CHICKEN WITH CHOY SUM

700g single chicken breast fillets, sliced thinly
2 cloves garlic, crushed
1 tablespoon grated lemon rind
1 cup (150g) plain flour, approximately
2 eggs, beaten lightly
1 cup (150g) sesame seeds
1/3 cup (80ml) peanut oil
250g choy sum, chopped

• Combine chicken with garlic and rind in large bowl, cover; refrigerate 3 hours or overnight.

• Dip chicken in flour, shake away excess; dip chicken in egg then, using hand, press on seeds. Place chicken on tray, cover; refrigerate at least 30 minutes.

To cook Heat oil in wok; stir-fry chicken, in batches, until browned and cooked through. Drain on absorbent paper.

• Return chicken to wok with choy sum; stir-fry, tossing until choy sum just wilts.

• Serve chicken mixture sprinkled with lemon wedges, if desired.

SERVES 4

CARIBBEAN GLAZED CHICKEN AND GREEN BEANS

400g green beans, halved
2 tablespoons peanut oil
1kg single chicken breast fillets, sliced thinly
2 large (600g) red onions, sliced
4 cloves garlic, crushed
3 bird's-eye chillies, seeded, chopped finely
300g tat soi, chopped
1/4 cup (65g) finely chopped palm sugar
1/4 cup (60ml) balsamic vinegar
1/4 cup (60ml) sweet chilli sauce

• Boil, steam or microwave beans until just tender; drain.

• Heat oil in wok; stir-fry chicken, onion, garlic and chilli, in batches, until chicken is browned and cooked through.

• Return chicken mixture and beans to wok with tat soi and combined remaining ingredients; stir-fry, tossing until tat soi is just wilted.

SERVES 4 TO 6

WARM CABBAGE AND ASPARAGUS SALAD

500g Hokkien noodles
1/3 cup (80ml) olive oil
1 medium (150g) white
** onion, chopped**
2 cloves garlic, crushed
1/3 cup (50g) pine nuts
2 teaspoons caraway seeds
500g asparagus, sliced
700g Chinese cabbage, shredded

1 tablespoon Dijon mustard
2 tablespoons balsamic vinegar
1 teaspoon brown sugar

• Rinse noodles under hot water; drain. Transfer noodles to large bowl; separate with fork.

• Heat 1 tablespoon of the oil in wok; stir-fry onion, garlic, nuts and seeds until onion is browned lightly.

• Add asparagus to wok; stir-fry, tossing until just tender.

• Add noodles, cabbage and combined remaining oil, mustard, vinegar and sugar to wok; stir-fry, tossing to combine with asparagus mixture.

SERVES 4

Above left Sesame chicken with choy sum
Below left Caribbean glazed chicken and green beans
Above Warm cabbage and asparagus salad

CHIVE AND FENNEL MEATBALLS WITH SAGE PESTO

500g minced pork
1/2 cup chopped fresh chives
3 cloves garlic, crushed
2 teaspoons ground fennel
1/4 cup (60ml) peanut oil
300g fresh thin egg noodles
2 medium (340g) red onions, sliced
2 cloves garlic, crushed, extra
1/4 cup (60ml) chicken stock
1 tablespoon hoisin sauce
1 tablespoon sweet chilli sauce
2 cups (160g) bean sprouts
200g baby spinach leaves

SAGE PESTO
2 cups loosely packed fresh
    sage leaves
1/2 cup (125ml) olive oil
2 tablespoons finely grated
    lemon rind
2 teaspoons sugar

COCONUT LIME-CURED FISH WITH CURLY GREENS

800g blue eye fillet
1/2 cup (125ml) lime juice
1 cup (250ml) coconut milk
1 tablespoon grated fresh ginger
1 small (200g) leek
2 tablespoons peanut oil
1 medium (150g) white
    onion, chopped
4 kaffir lime leaves, sliced
1 tablespoon grated fresh
    ginger, extra
1 medium (200g) red
    capsicum, sliced
60g curly endive
60g mizuna

• Cut fish into 5cm-square pieces; place in large bowl with juice, milk and ginger; mix well. Cover; refrigerate overnight.

To cook Halve leek lengthways, cut into 5cm pieces; cut pieces into thin strips.

• Drain fish; discard marinade.

• Heat 1/2 of the oil in wok; stir-fry fish with onion, lime leaves and extra ginger, in batches, until fish is cooked as desired.

• Heat remaining oil in same wok; stir-fry capsicum and leek until tender. Return fish mixture to wok; stir-fry, tossing to combine ingredients.

• Toss fish mixture in large bowl with endive and mizuna.

SERVES 4

- Using hand, combine pork, chives, garlic and fennel in medium bowl; roll level tablespoons of mixture into meatballs. *[Can be made ahead. Cover; refrigerate overnight or freeze.]*

To cook Heat 1/2 of the oil in wok; stir-fry meatballs, in batches, until browned all over and cooked through.

- Cook noodles in large pan of boiling water, uncovered, until just tender; drain. Cover to keep warm.

- Heat remaining oil in same wok; stir-fry onion and extra garlic until onion is browned lightly.

- Return meatballs to wok, add stock and sauces; stir-fry until sauce boils.

- Add sprouts and spinach to wok; stir-fry, tossing with meatball mixture, until spinach is just wilted.

- Serve meatballs on noodles; top with Sage Pesto.

Sage Pesto Blend or process all ingredients until mixture forms a paste; refrigerate, covered, until required.

SERVES 4

LAMB IN BASIL LEAVES WITH SESAME AIOLI

700g lamb eye of loin, sliced thinly
2 cups chopped fresh basil leaves
1/4 cup (60ml) olive oil
1 medium (150g) brown onion, sliced
150g tat soi, chopped

SESAME AIOLI
2 egg yolks
1 tablespoon Dijon mustard
1 tablespoon white wine vinegar
1 clove garlic, crushed
1 cup (250ml) olive oil
2 tablespoons hot water
1 tablespoon sesame seeds, toasted

- Combine lamb, basil and 1 tablespoon of the oil in large bowl, cover; refrigerate 3 hours or overnight.

To cook Heat remaining oil in wok; stir-fry lamb mixture and onion, in batches, until lamb is browned and cooked as desired. Wipe wok with absorbent paper.

- Stir-fry tat soi in same wok until crisp.

- Serve lamb mixture with tat soi and Sesame Aioli.

Sesame Aioli Blend or process egg yolks, mustard, vinegar and garlic until creamy. With motor operating, gradually add oil. Place aioli mixture in small bowl; stir in the hot water and seeds. Cover; refrigerate aioli 3 hours or overnight.

SERVES 4

Far left Coconut lime-cured fish with curly greens
Left Chive and fennel meatballs with sage pesto
Above Lamb in basil leaves with sesame aioli

PORK AND SNAKE BEANS MADRAS

4 bacon rashers, chopped
1 tablespoon peanut oil
700g pork fillets, sliced thinly
1 large (200g) white onion, sliced
1/4 cup (60g) Madras curry paste
200g snake beans, chopped
1/2 cup (125ml) beef stock
1 tablespoon tomato paste

• In dry heated wok, stir-fry bacon until crisp; drain on absorbent paper.

• Heat oil in same wok; stir-fry pork and onion, in batches, until browned.

• Stir-fry curry paste in same wok until just fragrant.

• Add snake beans to wok with pork mixture, bacon, stock and paste; stir-fry, tossing until sauce boils.

SERVES 4

COCONUT CURRIED DUCK

1/2 cup firmly packed fresh
  coriander leaves
4 bird's-eye chillies, seeded,
  chopped finely
1 tablespoon finely chopped fresh
  lemon grass
2 cloves garlic, crushed
1 tablespoon grated fresh ginger
2 teaspoons ground cumin
1 teaspoon garam masala
1/4 cup (60ml) peanut oil
600g duck breast fillets,
  sliced thinly
1 large (200g) brown onion, sliced
1 tablespoon tomato paste
1 2/3 cups (400ml) coconut cream
1 tablespoon fish sauce
2 tablespoons lime juice
2 tablespoons brown sugar
200g cherry tomatoes
500g choy sum, chopped

• Using blender or mortar and pestle, process coriander, chilli, lemon grass, garlic, ginger, cumin and garam masala with oil until mixture forms a paste.

• In dry heated wok, stir-fry duck and onion, in batches, until duck is browned and cooked through.

* Stir-fry curry paste in same wok until just fragrant.

* Return duck mixture to wok with tomato paste, cream, sauce, juice and sugar; stir-fry until sauce boils.

* Add tomatoes and choy sum; stir-fry, tossing until choy sum is just wilted.

SERVES 4

Left Pork and snake beans Madras
Below Coconut curried duck

BEETROOT AND TUNA SALAD

600g fresh belly tuna, chopped
1/2 cup chopped fresh dill
2 cloves garlic, crushed
1/4 cup (60ml) peanut oil
500g baby beetroot
300g curly endive

WASABI MAYONNAISE
2 egg yolks
2 teaspoons wasabi
1 tablespoon finely grated lime rind
2 tablespoons lime juice
1/2 cup (125ml) peanut oil
1 tablespoon hot water

• Combine tuna with dill, garlic and 1/2 of the oil in large bowl, cover; refrigerate 3 hours or overnight.

To cook Discard beetroot leaves and stems. Boil, steam or microwave until tender; drain. Peel beetroot while warm.

• Heat remaining oil in wok; stir-fry tuna mixture until cooked as desired.

• Combine beetroot with tuna and endive in large bowl; drizzle with mayonnaise.

Wasabi Mayonnaise Blend or process egg yolks, wasabi, rind and juice until smooth. With motor operating, gradually add oil; process until thick. Place mayonnaise in small bowl; stir in the hot water. Cover; refrigerate 3 hours or overnight.

SERVES 4

LAMB AND BUTTER BEAN GREEN CURRY

700g lamb fillets, sliced thinly
2 tablespoons peanut oil
1/3 cup (90g) green curry paste
1 medium (150g) brown onion, sliced
3 medium (360g) zucchini, sliced
2 x 400g cans butter beans,
    rinsed, drained
1 cup (250ml) coconut cream
1 tablespoon shredded fresh
    basil leaves

• Combine lamb, 1/2 of the oil and curry paste in large bowl, cover; refrigerate 3 hours or overnight.

To cook Heat remaining oil in wok; stir-fry lamb mixture and onion, in batches, until lamb is browned.

• Stir-fry zucchini and butter beans in same wok until just tender. Remove from wok.

• Return lamb mixture to wok with cream; stir-fry, tossing until sauce boils.

• Serve curry, tossing basil through off the heat, with zucchini and butter beans.

SERVES 4

LEMON CHICKEN WITH CRISP GOW GEE WRAPPERS

1 tablespoon peanut oil
700g chicken tenderloins, halved
2 bird's-eye chillies, seeded, chopped finely
1 clove garlic, crushed
8 gow gee pastry wrappers
1 egg white
1 tablespoon black sesame seeds
vegetable oil, for deep-frying
1/2 cup (125ml) chicken stock
2 teaspoons honey
1 tablespoon cornflour
1/2 cup (125ml) lemon juice
4 green onions, sliced

• Heat peanut oil in wok; stir-fry chicken, chilli and garlic, in batches, until chicken is browned and cooked through. Wipe wok clean with absorbent paper.

• Place pastry wrappers on tray in single layer; brush with egg white, sprinkle with sesame seeds.

• Heat vegetable oil in same wok; deep-fry wrappers, 1 at a time, until puffed and browned lightly. Drain crisp wrappers on absorbent paper. Discard cooled oil; wipe wok clean with absorbent paper.

• Return chicken mixture to wok with stock, honey and blended cornflour and juice; stir-fry, tossing until sauce boils.

• Serve chicken, tossing onion through off the heat, sandwiched between crisp gow gee wrappers.

SERVES 4

Above left Beetroot and tuna salad
Below left Lamb and butter bean green curry
Below Lemon chicken with crisp gow gee wrappers

DEVILLED PRAWN AND PASTA MELANGE

1kg uncooked tiger prawns
1 tablespoon sambal oelek
2 tablespoons olive oil
500g vermicelli
1/2 cup (35g) stale breadcrumbs
1/4 cup (60ml) lime juice
4 green onions, chopped
1/2 cup firmly packed chopped fresh coriander leaves

• Shell and devein prawns, leaving tails intact. Combine prawns, sambal and 1/2 of the oil in large bowl, cover; refrigerate 3 hours or overnight.

To cook Cook pasta in large pan of boiling water, uncovered, until just tender; drain. Cover to keep warm.

• Heat remaining oil in wok; stir-fry breadcrumbs until browned lightly. Remove from wok.

• Stir-fry prawns, in batches, in same wok until prawns are just changed in colour.

• Return prawns to wok with pasta, juice, onion, coriander and 1/2 of the breadcrumbs; stir-fry, tossing to combine.

• Serve prawn mixture sprinkled with remaining breadcrumbs.

SERVES 4

SUGAR SNAP AND SNOW PEAS WITH TOFU AND PISTACHIOS

2 tablespoons peanut oil
600g firm tofu, chopped
1 cup (150g) pistachios
30g butter
2 cloves garlic, crushed
2 bird's-eye chillies, seeded, chopped
2 teaspoons grated fresh ginger
400g sugar snap peas
400g snow peas
1/4 cup (60ml) sweet chilli sauce

• Heat 1/2 of the oil in wok; stir-fry tofu and nuts, in batches, until tofu is browned lightly.

• Heat remaining oil with butter in same wok; stir-fry garlic, chilli and ginger until mixture is fragrant.

• Add sugar snap and snow peas to wok; stir-fry until just tender.

• Return tofu and nuts to wok with sauce; stir-fry, tossing to combine ingredients.

SERVES 4

Left Devilled prawn and pasta melange
Right Sugar snap and snow peas with tofu and pistachios

LAMB'S FRY WITH FRIED NOODLES AND PANCETTA

800g lamb's fry
1/3 cup (80ml) peanut oil
120g thinly sliced pancetta
1 tablespoon sesame oil
400g fresh egg noodles
2 bird's-eye chillies, seeded, chopped finely
6 green onions, sliced lengthways
3 cloves garlic, crushed
1/2 cup (75g) plain flour, approximately
1/4 cup (60ml) sweet chilli sauce
1 tablespoon Worcestershire sauce
1/4 cup (60ml) beef stock

• Remove and discard membrane from lamb's fry. Soak lamb's fry in cold water 30 minutes; drain, pat dry with absorbent paper, slice thinly.

• Heat 1 tablespoon of the peanut oil in wok; stir-fry pancetta, in batches, until crisp. Drain on absorbent paper.

• Heat 1 tablespoon of remaining peanut oil with sesame oil in same wok; stir-fry noodles, chilli, onion and garlic, in batches, until noodles are browned lightly.

• Dip lamb's fry in flour; shake away excess. Heat remaining peanut oil in same wok; stir-fry lamb's fry, in batches, until just browned.

• Return lamb's fry and noodle mixture to wok with combined remaining ingredients; stir-fry, tossing until sauce boils.

• Serve lamb's fry and noodles topped with pancetta.

SERVES 4 TO 6

FRAGRANT BEEF WITH MINT AND CUCUMBER SALAD

700g beef steak, sliced thinly
6 star-anise, ground finely
1 tablespoon Sichuan peppercorns, ground finely
1 clove garlic, crushed
2 bird's-eye chillies, seeded, chopped finely
4 kaffir lime leaves, sliced
1 tablespoon peanut oil

MINT AND CUCUMBER SALAD
4 (520g) Lebanese cucumbers, peeled, sliced
1 clove garlic, crushed
1 tablespoon rice wine vinegar
1 bird's-eye chilli, seeded, chopped
1 tablespoon peanut oil
1 tablespoon lime juice
2 teaspoons sugar
100g watercress

1 cup chopped fresh mint leaves
**1 medium (170g) red
    onion, chopped**

• Combine beef, star-anise, pepper, garlic, chilli and lime leaves in large bowl, cover; refrigerate 3 hours or overnight.

To cook Heat oil in wok; stir-fry beef mixture, in batches, until browned.

• Serve beef with salad.

Mint and Cucumber Salad Combine cucumber, garlic, vinegar, chilli, oil, juice and sugar in large bowl, cover; refrigerate about 1 hour or until cucumber softens. Just before serving, add watercress, mint and onion to bowl; toss to combine.

SERVES 4

CRISPY DUCK AND CREAMY SPINACH RISOTTO

1¹/₂ cups (300g) jasmine rice
1 tablespoon olive oil
**600g duck breast fillets,
    sliced thinly**
**1 large (200g) white
    onion, chopped**
1 clove garlic, crushed
¹/₂ cup (125ml) chicken stock
¹/₂ cup (125ml) cream
**2 teaspoons finely grated
    lemon rind**
500g spinach, trimmed, chopped
¹/₄ cup chopped fresh chives
¹/₄ cup (60ml) lemon juice

• Cook rice in large pan of boiling water, uncovered, until just tender; drain.

• Heat oil in wok; stir-fry duck, onion and garlic, in batches, until duck is browned and cooked through. Wipe wok clean with absorbent paper.

• Stir-fry rice in same wok with stock, cream, rind, spinach and chives until spinach is just wilted. Stir through juice.

• Serve duck on risotto.

SERVES 4 TO 6

Above left Lamb's fry with fried noodles and pancetta
Below left Fragrant beef with mint and cucumber salad
Right Crispy duck and creamy spinach risotto

Flights of fancy

By now you can see that there's more to stir-frying than just tossing a few cups of chopped vegetables together in a wok with a little soy, garlic and ginger. Take this dish (you'll find the recipe on page 98) as a case in point: its origins could be in Melbourne, Manhattan, Malaysia or a combination of all three, but it makes a single mouthwatering statement: the scope of food you can cook in your wok is only bound by the borders of your imagination. And the real beauty of taking a culinary trip courtesy of your wok is that you'll be preparing meals that are simple but innovative, healthy yet succulent, quick to make yet timeless in their appeal.

SALMON AND SOBA WITH NORI PESTO

700g salmon steaks, cut into 2cm pieces
500g soba
1 sheet toasted nori
1 tablespoon olive oil

NORI PESTO
1 sheet toasted nori, shredded
3/4 cup firmly packed fresh basil leaves
1/4 cup firmly packed fresh dill
2 tablespoons pine nuts
1 clove garlic, crushed
1/2 cup (125ml) olive oil
1/4 cup (20g) coarsely grated parmesan cheese

• Combine salmon with 1/2 of the Nori Pesto in large bowl, cover; refrigerate 3 hours.

To cook Cook soba in large pan of boiling water, uncovered, until just tender; drain.

• Cut nori sheet into 5mm-wide pieces.

• Drain salmon; discard marinade. Heat oil in wok; stir-fry salmon, in batches, until browned and cooked as desired.

• Stir-fry soba in same wok until hot; add salmon and nori, toss until combined.

• Toss remaining Nori Pesto through the salmon mixture off the heat.

Nori Pesto Blend or process all ingredients until combined.

SERVES 4 TO 6

WARM BEETROOT AND MACADAMIA SALAD

8 medium (1.4kg) beetroots
40g ghee
2 small (400g) leeks, sliced
1 cup (150g) macadamias
1/4 cup (60ml) raspberry vinegar
1/4 cup (60ml) olive oil
1 clove garlic, crushed
250g baby rocket leaves
250g baby spinach leaves
150g goat cheese, crumbled

• Boil, steam or microwave beetroot until tender; drain. Peel beetroot while warm; cut into wedges.

• Heat ghee in wok; stir-fry leek and nuts until leek is soft and nuts are heated browned lightly.

• Add beetroot, vinegar, oil and garlic to wok; stir-fry, tossing until beetroot are heated through.

• Toss rocket, spinach and cheese through beetroot mixture off the heat.

SERVES 4 TO 6

Glass plate from Accoutrement

Left Salmon and soba with nori pesto
Right Warm beetroot and macadamia salad

CRISPY DUCK WITH PORT-MACERATED FIGS

250g dried figs
1/2 cup (125ml) port
2 tablespoons brown sugar
600g duck breast fillets
1/3 cup (50g) cornflour,
    approximately
1 tablespoon peanut oil
1 medium (150g) white
    onion, sliced
2 cloves garlic, crushed
1 tablespoon chopped fresh thyme
80g snow pea sprouts
150g watercress

• Cut figs in half; combine in small bowl with port and sugar. Cover; stand 3 hours or overnight.

To cook Cut each duck fillet in half; coat with cornflour, shake away excess.

• Heat oil in wok; stir-fry duck, in batches, until crisp and cooked through. Drain duck on absorbent paper; cover to keep warm.

• Drain excess oil from wok; stir-fry onion and garlic until onion is soft.

• Add undrained fig mixture; stir-fry until sauce boils.

• Return duck to wok; stir-fry, tossing until ingredients are combined.

• Serve the duck mixture with combined thyme, sprouts and watercress.

SERVES 4

LAMB CHERMOULLA

700g lamb eye of loin, sliced thinly
1/2 cup chopped fresh parsley
1 tablespoon grated lemon rind
1 tablespoon grated lime rind
1 tablespoon lemon juice
1 tablespoon lime juice
2 teaspoons ground turmeric
1 teaspoon ground cayenne pepper
1 tablespoon ground cumin
1 tablespoon ground coriander
2 tablespoons peanut oil
1 medium (170g) red
    onion, chopped

• Combine all ingredients in large bowl, cover; refrigerate 3 hours or overnight.

To cook Stir-fry lamb mixture, in batches, until browned and cooked as desired.

• Serve Lamb Chermoulla with tabouleh and hummus, if desired.

SERVES 4

Resin plate from Dinosaur Designs; napkin from Accoutrement

Left Crispy duck with port-macerated figs
Above Lamb chermoulla

Plates and chopsticks from Empire Homewares

CHILLI BEEF 'N' BEANS IN RADICCHIO CUPS

We used a 200g jar of mild taco sauce in this recipe but, since some like it hot, you can use the medium or hot versions if you prefer.

1 medium (250g) avocado
2 tablespoons lime juice
1 small (100g) red onion, chopped
1 small (130g) tomato, seeded, chopped
1 tablespoon olive oil
500g minced beef
1 medium (150g) brown onion, chopped
2 cloves garlic, crushed
2 teaspoons ground coriander
1 bird's-eye chilli, seeded, chopped finely
200g jar taco sauce
290g can kidney beans, rinsed, drained
1 medium (200g) radicchio
1/2 cup (125ml) sour cream

- Mash avocado flesh in small bowl until almost smooth; stir in juice, red onion and tomato. Cover avocado mixture; refrigerate.

- Heat oil in wok; stir-fry beef, brown onion, garlic, coriander and chilli, in batches, until beef is browned.

- Add sauce and beans; stir-fry, tossing until sauce boils.

- Spoon mixture into radicchio leaves; top with sour cream and avocado mixture.

SERVES 4

WARM BEEF SALAD

500g beef steak, sliced thinly
1 tablespoon olive oil
1 tablespoon ground cumin
1 tablespoon ground coriander
1 tablespoon lemon juice
2 cloves garlic, crushed
2 large pitta breads
1 tablespoon olive oil, extra
2 medium (340g) red onions, sliced
4 medium (300g) egg tomatoes
250g baby rocket leaves
200g yogurt
1 tablespoon chopped fresh mint leaves
1 tablespoon lemon juice, extra
1 clove garlic, crushed, extra

- Combine beef, oil, cumin, coriander, juice and garlic in large bowl, cover; refrigerate 3 hours or overnight.

To cook Place pitta on oven tray in moderate oven about 5 minutes or until browned lightly and crisp; cool, break into pieces.

- Heat extra oil in wok; stir-fry beef mixture and onion, in batches, until beef is browned.

- Cut tomatoes into wedges; stir-fry in same wok until just hot.

- Return beef mixture to wok; stir-fry to combine with tomato.

- Serve beef mixture on top of rocket, accompanied by pitta and combined remaining ingredients.

SERVES 4

Left Warm beef salad
Right Chilli beef 'n' beans in radicchio cups

PEPPER-CREAM VEGETABLES

1 tablespoon olive oil
2 medium (300g) brown
    onions, sliced
2 medium (240g) carrots, sliced
4 baby (240g) eggplants, sliced
1 clove garlic, crushed
250g button mushrooms, halved
2 medium (240g) zucchini, sliced
1 medium (200g) red
    capsicum, sliced
1/2 cup (125ml) water
1/2 cup (125ml) cream
1 vegetable stock cube
2 tablespoons cracked black pepper

• Heat oil in wok, stir-fry all vegetables, in batches, until just tender.

• Add combined water, cream, crumbled stock cube and pepper to same wok; stir until sauce thickens slightly.

• Serve vegetables with sauce.

SERVES 4

TUNISIAN-STYLE BEEF

2 cloves garlic, crushed
2 teaspoons grated fresh ginger
1/4 cup (60ml) orange juice
1 tablespoon white wine vinegar
2 teaspoons ground coriander
1 teaspoon mixed spice
1/2 cup (100g) couscous
1/2 cup (125ml) boiling water
20g butter
2 tablespoons olive oil
1 medium (170g) red
    onion, chopped
4 medium (760g) tomatoes,
    seeded, chopped
1/4 cup chopped fresh mint leaves
1/4 cup chopped fresh parsley
2 tablespoons lemon juice

• Combine beef, garlic, ginger, orange juice, vinegar, coriander and mixed spice in large bowl, cover; refrigerate 3 hours or overnight.

To cook Combine couscous, the boiling water and butter in medium heatproof bowl; cover, stand about 5 minutes or until water is absorbed. Using fork, stir couscous to separate grains.

• Heat 1/2 of the oil in wok; stir-fry the beef mixture and onion, in batches, until beef is browned.

• Heat remaining oil in wok; stir-fry tomato until hot. Return beef mixture to wok with couscous, mint, parsley and lemon juice; stir-fry, tossing to combine.

SERVES 4

Left Pepper-cream vegetables
Above Tunisian-style beef

MEXICAN-STYLE WHITE BEANS AND CHORIZO

2 tablespoons olive oil
5 (650g) chorizo sausages, sliced
1 medium (170g) red onion, sliced
3 cloves garlic, crushed
4 medium (300g) egg
   tomatoes, chopped

2 x 400g cans cannellini beans,
   rinsed, drained
1/2 cup (80g) black olives, seeded
1/4 cup firmly packed fresh
   basil leaves
2 tablespoons chopped fresh parsley
2 tablespoons red wine vinegar
1/2 teaspoon sugar

• Heat 1/2 of the oil in wok; stir-fry chorizo, in batches, until browned. Drain on absorbent paper.

• Drain excess oil from wok; stir-fry onion and garlic until onion is soft.

• Add about 3/4 of the tomato to same wok; stir-fry until tomato is soft.

• Return chorizo to wok with beans, olives, herbs, vinegar and sugar; stir-fry, tossing until hot.

• Serve chorizo and beans topped with remaining tomato.

SERVES 4

PRAWNS IN BASIL WITH AVOCADO MASH

1kg uncooked tiger prawns
1/2 cup chopped fresh basil leaves
2 cloves garlic, crushed
1 tablespoon finely grated lime rind
2 tablespoons peanut oil

AVOCADO MASH
2 medium (500g) avocados
2 tablespoons lime juice
2 medium (380g) tomatoes,
   seeded, chopped
1 small (100g) red onion, chopped
2 teaspoons ground cumin
2 tablespoons chopped fresh
   basil leaves
2 bird's-eye chillies, seeded,
   chopped finely

• Shell and devein prawns, leaving tails intact. Combine prawns in large bowl with basil, garlic and rind; cover; refrigerate 3 hours or overnight.

To cook Heat oil in wok; stir-fry prawns until just changed in colour.

• Serve prawns over Avocado Mash.

Avocado Mash Mash flesh of 1 avocado in small bowl until almost smooth. Chop flesh of second avocado roughly; add to bowl of mashed avocado with remaining ingredients, mix well.

SERVES 4

Left Mexican-style white beans and chorizo
Right Prawns in basil with avocado mash

PANCETTA, PARMESAN AND SPINACH SALAD

1/3 cup (80ml) olive oil
300g thin slices pancetta, chopped
1 medium (170g) red onion, chopped
6 slices white bread
2 cloves garlic, crushed
100g parmesan cheese
500g baby spinach leaves
1 tablespoon balsamic vinegar

• Heat 1 tablespoon of the oil in wok; stir-fry pancetta and onion, in batches, until crisp. Drain on absorbent paper.

• Remove and discard crusts from bread; cut bread into 2cm pieces. Place in medium bowl with garlic and 1 tablespoon of the remaining oil; mix well.

• Heat 1 tablespoon of the remaining oil in same wok. Stir-fry bread, in batches, until croutons are golden brown; drain on absorbent paper.

• Using vegetable peeler, shave cheese into thin strips.

• Toss pancetta mixture and croutons in large bowl with spinach and combined remaining oil and vinegar; sprinkle cheese over the top.

SERVES 4

SWEET AND CRUNCHY PORK IN WITLOF CUPS

1/2 cup (125ml) maple syrup
500g pork fillets, sliced thinly
1/4 cup (60ml) lemon juice
2 cloves garlic, crushed
1 tablespoon cider vinegar
1 teaspoon seeded mustard
1/3 cup (80ml) olive oil
1/2 cup (40g) slivered
    almonds, toasted
4 (500g) witlof

• Reserve 2 teaspoons of the maple syrup. Combine remaining syrup in large bowl with pork, juice and garlic, cover; refrigerate 3 hours or overnight.

To cook Drain pork; discard marinade.

• Combine reserved syrup, vinegar, mustard and 1/4 cup of the oil in small jug.

• Heat remaining oil in wok; stir-fry pork, in batches, until browned. Return pork to wok with syrup mixture; stir-fry, tossing until sauce boils.

• Toss nuts through pork mixture off the heat; serve spooned into witlof leaves.

SERVES 4

Left Pancetta, parmesan and spinach salad
Right Sweet and crunchy pork in witlof cups

SCALLOPS WITH PROSCIUTTO AND FRESH HERBS

1kg scallops
1/4 cup chopped fresh dill
1/4 cup chopped fresh garlic chives
3 bird's-eye chillies, seeded,
** chopped finely**
2 tablespoons finely grated lime rind
1/4 cup (60ml) vodka
1 tablespoon raw sugar
2 tablespoons olive oil
12 slices (180g) prosciutto
2 tablespoons sweet chilli sauce

• Combine scallops with dill, chives, chilli, rind, vodka, sugar and 1/2 of the oil in large bowl, cover; refrigerate 3 hours or overnight.

To cook Stir-fry prosciutto, in batches, in dry heated wok until browned and crisp.

• Drain scallops over medium bowl; reserve marinade.

• Heat remaining oil in wok; stir-fry scallops, in batches, until tender.

• Return scallop mixture to wok with reserved marinade and chilli sauce; stir until liquid boils.

• Serve scallops, topped with prosciutto, with fresh egg noodles, if desired.

SERVES 4 TO 6

WARM CHICKEN, ROCKET AND FETTA SALAD

700g single chicken breast fillets,
** sliced thinly**
4 cloves garlic, crushed
1/2 cup (125ml) olive oil
1 large (300g) red onion, sliced
1 cup (150g) drained
** sun-dried tomatoes**
200g fetta cheese, chopped
1/4 cup (60ml) balsamic vinegar
1 tablespoon honey
500g rocket, trimmed

• Combine the chicken, garlic and 1 tablespoon of the oil in large bowl, cover; refrigerate 1 hour or overnight.

To cook Heat 1 tablespoon of remaining oil in wok; stir-fry chicken and onion, in batches, until browned.

• Return chicken mixture to wok with tomatoes, cheese and

Left Scallops with prosciutto and fresh herbs
Right Warm chicken, rocket and fetta salad

EGGPLANT AND SALSA FRESCA

10 baby (600g) eggplants
2 tablespoons peanut oil
1 medium (150g) white onion, sliced
2 cloves garlic, crushed
1 teaspoon sambal oelek
1 cup (250ml) tomato juice
6 green onions, chopped

SALSA FRESCA
1 (130g) Lebanese cucumber
1 large (250g) tomato, seeded, chopped
1 trimmed (75g) stick celery, chopped finely
1/4 teaspoon Tabasco sauce
1 tablespoon lime juice

• Halve eggplants lengthways; cut 4 long strips through each piece lengthways, stopping about 1cm from stem end.

• Heat 1/2 of the oil in wok; stir-fry eggplant, in batches, until just browned.

• Heat remaining oil in same wok; stir-fry white onion, garlic and sambal. Return eggplant to wok with juice; stir-fry until eggplant is tender.

• Serve eggplant mixture topped with Salsa Fresca and green onion.

Salsa Fresca Halve cucumber lengthways; remove and discard seeds, chop flesh in small dice. Combine cucumber in small bowl with remaining ingredients.

SERVES 4

SATURDAY NIGHT SAUSAGE SUPPER

We used the small, finger-shaped kipfler potato in this recipe but you can use any small potato you wish.

500g kipfler potatoes
12 (800g) lamb sausages
4 bacon rashers, chopped
2 tablespoons olive oil
2 large (400g) brown onions, sliced
2 cloves garlic, crushed
1 tablespoon seeded mustard
1 tablespoon chopped fresh chives
300ml sour cream

• Boil, steam or microwave potatoes until tender; drain.

• Cook sausages in large pan of boiling water, uncovered, about 4 minutes or until just changed in colour. Drain sausages; cut into thin slices.

• Stir-fry bacon in dry heated wok until crisp; remove from wok.

• Heat oil in same wok; stir-fry potato, sausage, onion and garlic, in batches, until browned.

• Return sausage mixture to wok with bacon, mustard, chives and sour cream; stir-fry, tossing until hot.

SERVES 4

Far left Eggplant and salsa fresca
Left Saturday night sausage supper

Glasses from Shack, plate from Empire Homewares

Above Chilli lime green-bean trio
Top right Lamb Roman-style
Right Quick-as-a-flash sausages and beans

CHILLI LIME GREEN-BEAN TRIO

1 tablespoon olive oil
250g snake beans, sliced
350g frozen broad beans,
thawed, peeled
350g green beans

CHILLI LIME DRESSING
1 tablespoon olive oil
2 teaspoons grated lime rind
2 tablespoons lime juice
1/2 teaspoon sambal oelek
1 teaspoon chopped fresh
mint leaves
1 tablespoon chopped fresh
basil leaves
1 clove garlic, crushed

• Heat oil in wok; stir-fry all beans, in batches, until tender.

• Return beans to wok with 1/2 of the Chilli Lime Dressing; stir until hot.

• Just before serving, combine bean mixture with remaining Chilli Lime Dressing in large bowl.

Chilli Lime Dressing Combine all ingredients in jar; shake well.

SERVES 4

LAMB ROMAN-STYLE

1 cup (200g) dried borlotti beans
1 cup (150g) sun-dried
tomatoes in oil
2 tablespoons chopped
fresh oregano
1 tablespoon chopped
fresh marjoram
4 cloves garlic, crushed
2 tablespoons balsamic vinegar
1kg lamb eye of loin, sliced thinly
30g butter
250g button mushrooms, sliced
2 medium (300g) brown
onions, chopped
2 tablespoons chopped fresh
oregano, extra
1/4 cup (60ml) beef stock

• Cover beans with water in large bowl; refrigerate overnight.

• Drain tomatoes over small bowl; reserve oil. Chop tomatoes, cover; refrigerate.

• Combine reserved oil with herbs, garlic, vinegar and lamb in large bowl, cover; refrigerate 3 hours or overnight.

To cook Drain beans, rinse; cook in large pan of boiling water, uncovered, about 1 hour or until beans are tender. Drain.

• Heat butter in wok; stir-fry mushrooms until browned lightly, remove from wok.

• Stir-fry lamb mixture and onion in same wok, in batches, until lamb is browned.

• Return lamb mixture to wok with beans, mushrooms, extra oregano, tomato and stock; stir-fry, tossing until sauce boils.

SERVES 6

QUICK-AS-A-FLASH
SAUSAGES AND BEANS

1 tablespoon olive oil
1kg beef chipolata sausages
2 large (400g) brown onions, sliced
2 cloves garlic, crushed
6 large (540g) egg tomatoes
400g can cannellini beans,
rinsed, drained
1 tablespoon chopped fresh thyme

• Heat oil in wok; stir-fry sausages, onion and garlic, in batches, until sausages are browned and cooked through.

• Cut tomatoes into wedges; stir-fry in same wok with beans until just hot.

• Return sausage mixture to wok; stir-fry, tossing to combine ingredients.

• Serve sausage mixture with thyme scattered over top.

SERVES 6

HOT AND LEMONY GARLIC MUSSELS

1kg small black mussels
1½ cups (300g) couscous
1½ cups (375ml) boiling water
2 tablespoons olive oil
1 large (300g) red onion,
    chopped finely
½ cup chopped fresh parsley
½ teaspoon hot paprika
¼ teaspoon ground turmeric
¼ teaspoon chilli powder
1 teaspoon cracked black pepper
½ cup (125ml) lemon juice
3 cloves garlic, crushed
2 teaspoons Dijon mustard

• Scrub mussels and remove beards.

• Combine couscous and the boiling water in small heatproof bowl; cover, stand about 5 minutes or until water is absorbed. Using a fork, stir couscous to separate grains.

• Heat ½ of the oil in wok; stir-fry onion until soft.

• Add couscous, parsley, spices and pepper to wok; stir-fry, tossing until combined. Remove from wok; wipe wok clean with absorbent paper.

• Heat remaining oil in wok; stir-fry mussels, juice, garlic and mustard until sauce boils and mussels open (discard any that do not).

• Serve mussels tossed with couscous mixture in large bowl.

SERVES 4

SPAGHETTI PRIMAVERA WITH BASIL BUTTER

125g butter, softened
¼ cup chopped fresh basil leaves
500g spaghetti
1 medium (350g) leek, trimmed
1 large (150g) zucchini
1 tablespoon olive oil
1 medium (170g) red onion,
    chopped finely
2 cloves garlic, crushed
1 large (350g) red capsicum,
    sliced thinly
1 large (350g) yellow capsicum,
    sliced thinly
½ cup (80g) pine nuts, toasted
1 tablespoon basil leaves, torn

• Combine butter and chopped basil in small bowl; using plastic wrap as a guide, roll butter mixture into log shape. Refrigerate 30 minutes or overnight.

To cook Cut leek crossways into thirds; halve each piece lengthways, then cut halved pieces into thin strips. Repeat process with zucchini.

• Cook pasta in large pan of boiling water, uncovered, until just tender; drain. Cover to keep warm.

• Heat oil in wok; stir-fry onion and garlic until onion is soft. Add capsicum to wok; stir-fry until just browned.

• Add leek and zucchini to wok; stir-fry until leek is just soft.

• Place vegetables in large bowl with pasta; gently toss to combine.

• Sprinkle pasta mixture with thinly sliced basil butter, pine nuts and torn basil.

SERVES 4

Left Hot and lemony garlic mussels
Right Spaghetti primavera with basil butter

ASPARAGUS WITH CITRUS-TOASTED BREADCRUMBS

40g butter
2 tablespoons peanut oil
1¹/2 cups (105g) stale breadcrumbs
2 tablespoons finely grated
    orange rind
2 cloves garlic, crushed
750g asparagus, trimmed
8 sprigs fresh tarragon
1 cup (80g) flaked parmesan cheese

• Heat ¹/2 of the butter and ¹/2 of the peanut oil in wok; stir-fry combined breadcrumbs and rind until lightly browned, remove from wok.

• Heat remaining butter and oil in same wok; stir-fry garlic and asparagus, in batches, until asparagus is tender.

• Serve asparagus sprinkled with tarragon, breadcrumbs and cheese.

SERVES 4 TO 6

BALSAMIC BEEF WITH FENNEL AND FETTA

700g beef steak, sliced thinly
2 cloves garlic, crushed
1 teaspoon sugar
¹/2 cup (125ml) balsamic vinegar
¹/4 cup (60ml) olive oil
1 large (200g) brown onion, sliced
4 medium (760g) tomatoes,
    seeded, sliced
2 baby (340g) fennel, sliced
1 tablespoon chopped fresh
    mint leaves
1 tablespoon chopped fresh
    basil leaves
125g fetta cheese, crumbled

• Combine beef, garlic, sugar, ¹/2 of the vinegar and ¹/2 of the oil in large bowl, cover; refrigerate 3 hours or overnight.

To cook Heat ¹/2 of the remaining oil in wok; stir-fry beef mixture and onion, in batches, until beef is browned.

• Stir-fry tomato and fennel in same wok until fennel is just tender.

• Return beef mixture to wok with remaining vinegar and oil, mint and basil; stir-fry, tossing until combined.

• Serve, sprinkling cheese over beef mixture off the heat.

SERVES 4

Left Asparagus with citrus-toasted breadcrumbs
Right Balsamic beef with fennel and fetta

Bowls from Made in Japan

BUTTERFLIED PRAWNS IN CHERMOULLA

1kg large uncooked prawns
2 tablespoons olive oil
2 tablespoons dry white wine
1 cup (250ml) boiling water
1 cup (200g) couscous
40g butter

CHERMOULLA
1/3 cup chopped fresh parsley
1 tablespoon chopped fresh coriander leaves
1 teaspoon ground cumin
1/2 teaspoon sweet paprika
1 clove garlic, chopped
2 tablespoons grated lemon rind
1 tablespoon olive oil

• Shell prawns, leaving tails intact. Cut prawns down the back, not cutting all the way through; remove veins.

• Combine prawns with 1/2 of the Chermoulla, 1/2 of the oil and wine, cover; refrigerate 3 hours or overnight.

To cook Combine the boiling water and couscous in small heatproof bowl; cover, stand about 5 minutes or until water is absorbed. Using a fork, stir couscous to separate grains.

• Drain prawns; discard marinade.

• Heat remaining oil in wok; stir-fry prawns, in batches, until prawns are changed in colour.

• Heat butter in same wok; stir-fry couscous, tossing until hot. Remove from wok; cover to keep warm.

• Return prawns to wok with the remaining Chermoulla; stir-fry, tossing until combined.

• Serve prawns on top of couscous.

Chermoulla Blend or process all ingredients until mixture forms a paste.

SERVES 4 TO 6

BALSAMIC AND BASIL LAMB SALAD

700g lamb eye of loin, sliced thinly
1 cup finely chopped fresh basil leaves
1/3 cup (80ml) balsamic vinegar
1 clove garlic, crushed
1 tablespoon grated lemon rind
2 tablespoons peanut oil
200g cherry tomatoes
1 medium (200g) yellow capsicum, sliced
150g mesclun
1 medium (170g) red onion, sliced thinly
2 medium (280g) lemons, segmented
2 tablespoons balsamic vinegar
1/4 cup (60ml) olive oil
200g fetta cheese, crumbled
1 cup finely chopped fresh basil leaves, extra

• Combine lamb, basil, 1/2 of the vinegar, garlic and rind in large bowl, cover; refrigerate 3 hours or overnight.

To cook Heat 1/2 of the peanut oil in wok; stir-fry lamb mixture, in batches, until browned.

• Heat remaining peanut oil in same wok; stir-fry tomatoes and capsicum until capsicum is just tender.

• Combine lamb mixture, tomato and capsicum in large bowl with mesclun, onion and lemon; drizzle with combined extra basil, vinegar and olive oil.

• Serve lamb salad sprinkled with cheese.

SERVES 4

Above Balsamic and basil lamb salad
Right Butterflied prawns in chermoulla

SAUSAGE GENOVESE

12 thin (840g) beef sausages
1/2 cup firmly packed fresh basil
    leaves, chopped
1/4 cup (60ml) balsamic vinegar
2 cloves garlic, crushed
2 medium (300g) brown
    onions, sliced
2 teaspoons olive oil
200g mushrooms, halved
1/4 cup (60ml) dry red wine
1/2 cup firmly packed fresh basil
    leaves, chopped, extra

• Prick sausages all over, combine in large bowl with basil, 2 tablespoons of the vinegar, garlic and onion, cover; refrigerate 3 hours or overnight.

To cook Drain sausage mixture over medium bowl; reserve marinade.

• Heat oil in wok; stir-fry sausage mixture, in batches, until sausages are browned and cooked through. Cut sausages into thin slices.

• Stir-fry mushrooms in same wok until just tender.

• Return sausage mixture to wok with reserved marinade, remaining vinegar and wine; stir-fry, tossing until sauce boils.

• Serve, tossing extra basil through sausage mixture off the heat.

SERVES 4 TO 6

PORK WITH FRESH CITRUS AND MACADAMIAS

1 tablespoon peanut oil
450g pork fillets, sliced thinly
2 medium (400g) yellow
    capsicums, sliced
3 cloves garlic, crushed
1 tablespoon grated fresh ginger
1/4 cup (60ml) lemon juice
1/4 cup (60ml) lime juice
1/3 cup (80ml) orange juice
1 tablespoon sugar
1 teaspoon cornflour
1 tablespoon water
1 cup (150g) macadamias, halved
1 large (300g) orange, segmented
160g snow pea sprouts

• Heat 1/2 of the oil in wok; stir-fry pork, in batches, until browned.

• Heat remaining oil in same wok, stir-fry capsicum, garlic and ginger until capsicum is just tender.

• Return pork to wok with juices, sugar and blended cornflour and water; stir-fry, tossing until sauce boils. Remove pork mixture from heat; cover to keep warm.

• Stir-fry nuts and orange segments in wok until the nuts are browned lightly.

• Serve pork tossed with sprouts, nuts and orange segments.

SERVES 4

Far left Sausage Genovese
Left Pork with fresh citrus and macadamias

MIXED SEAFOOD SALAD

500g medium uncooked prawns
250g baby octopus
250g scallops
500g firm white fish
    fillets, chopped
1/3 cup (80ml) olive oil
1 clove garlic, crushed
1 large (300g) red onion, sliced
350g radishes, sliced
250g cherry tomatoes, halved
1 medium (200g) green
    capsicum, sliced
250g baby spinach leaves

MUSTARD YOGURT DRESSING
200ml yogurt
1 tablespoon seeded mustard
1 tablespoon lime juice
1 tablespoon water
1 clove garlic, crushed

• Shell and devein prawns, leaving tails intact. Remove and discard heads and beaks from octopus; cut each octopus into quarters.

• Combine prawns, octopus, scallops and fish in large bowl with 1/4 cup of the oil and garlic, cover; refrigerate seafood 3 hours or overnight.

To cook Heat remaining oil in wok; stir-fry seafood, in batches, until cooked as desired.

• Combine seafood in large bowl with onion, radish, tomato, capsicum and spinach. Pour over Mustard Yogurt Dressing; toss to combine.

Mustard Yogurt Dressing Combine all ingredients in small bowl; mix well.

SERVES 4 TO 6

AEGEAN BEEF WITH CAPERS AND HALOUMI

700g beef steak, sliced thinly
1 clove garlic, crushed
2 tablespoons capers,
    chopped finely
1 tablespoon finely grated
    lemon rind
1 tablespoon lemon juice
1/3 cup (80ml) olive oil
1 medium (150g) brown
    onion, chopped
500g asparagus
250g haloumi cheese, sliced
300g baby rocket leaves
1 tablespoon lemon juice, extra
1 tablespoon finely grated lemon
    rind, extra

• Combine beef, garlic, capers, rind and juice in large bowl, cover; refrigerate 3 hours or overnight.

To cook Heat 1/2 of the oil in wok; stir-fry beef mixture and onion, in batches, until beef is browned.

• Cut asparagus in half; stir-fry in same wok until just tender.

• Return beef mixture to wok with cheese; stir-fry until cheese starts to soften.

• Add rocket; stir-fry, tossing until rocket is just wilted.

• Serve beef mixture, drizzled with combined remaining oil and extra juice; sprinkle extra rind over the top.

SERVES 4

Left Mixed seafood salad
Right Aegean beef with capers and haloumi

MINTED PORK AND BEANS

700g pork fillets, sliced thinly
2 cloves garlic, crushed
2 tablespoons chopped fresh
**   mint leaves**
500g green beans, halved
2 tablespoons peanut oil
1 medium (170g) red
**   onion, chopped**
1 tablespoon lemon juice
80g butter
2 tablespoons chopped fresh mint
**   leaves, extra**

• Combine pork, garlic and mint in large bowl; cover; refrigerate 3 hours or overnight.

To cook Boil, steam or microwave beans until just tender; drain.

• Heat oil in wok; stir-fry pork mixture and onion, in batches, until browned.

• Return pork mixture to wok with beans, juice, butter and extra mint; stir-fry, tossing until hot.

• Serve pork and green bean mixture over warm noodles, if desired.

SERVES 4

WARM LAMB TABOULLEH

500g lamb eye of loin, sliced thinly
2 cloves garlic, crushed
1/4 cup (60ml) lemon juice
2 tablespoons olive oil
1 cup (160g) burghul
250g cherry tomatoes, halved
8 green onions, chopped
1/4 cup (60ml) lemon juice, extra
1/2 cup chopped fresh parsley
1/2 cup chopped fresh mint leaves

• Combine lamb, garlic, juice and 1/2 of the oil in large bowl, cover; refrigerate 3 hours or overnight.

To cook Cover burghul with cold water in small bowl; stand 15 minutes, drain. Rinse burghul under cold water; drain, squeeze out excess moisture.

• Heat remaining oil in wok; stir-fry lamb mixture, in batches, until browned. Cover.

• Stir-fry burghul, tomato and onion in same wok until onion is browned lightly.

• Toss extra juice, parsley and mint through taboulleh off the heat; serve with lamb mixture.

SERVES 4

Left Minted pork and beans
Below Warm lamb taboulleh

ATHENIAN LAMB, FETTA AND ARTICHOKES

500g lamb fillets, sliced thinly
2 tablespoons lemon juice
3 cloves garlic, crushed
1/3 cup (80ml) olive oil
500g tiny new potatoes, halved
1 large (300g) red onion, sliced
400g can artichoke hearts,
    drained, quartered
1 medium (140g) lemon,
    cut into wedges
2 tablespoons drained capers
1/2 cup (80g) black olives, seeded
100g fetta cheese, chopped
1 tablespoon chopped fresh
    mint leaves

• Combine lamb, juice, garlic and 1 tablespoon of the oil in large bowl, cover; refrigerate 3 hours or overnight.

To cook Boil, steam or microwave potatoes until just tender; drain.

• Heat 1/2 of the remaining oil in wok, stir-fry lamb mixture and onion, in batches, until lamb is browned.

• Heat remaining oil in same wok; stir-fry potatoes until browned. Add artichokes, lemon and capers; stir-fry until lemon begins to glaze.

• Return lamb mixture to wok; toss olives, cheese and mint through off the heat.

SERVES 4 TO 6

ARTICHOKES WITH FRIED NOODLES AND PEANUTS

4 medium (800g) globe artichokes
1/3 cup (80ml) lemon juice
2 1/2 cups (175g) stale breadcrumbs
5 cloves garlic, crushed
2 tablespoons finely grated
    lemon rind
1/3 cup (80ml) peanut oil
1/2 cup (75g) raw peanuts
500g thin fresh egg noodles
1 large (300g) red onion, chopped
2 bird's-eye chillies, seeded,
    chopped finely
1 cup (120g) seeded black
    olives, halved
2 tablespoons oyster sauce
1/4 cup (60ml) vegetable stock

• Trim stems from artichokes, remove tough outer leaves, trim tips of remaining leaves. Pull away some inside leaves, then scoop out the coarse centre with a spoon.

• Place artichokes and juice in large pan of boiling water; simmer, covered, about 30 minutes or until artichokes are tender. Drain; quarter artichokes.

• Combine breadcrumbs, garlic and rind in small bowl.

• Heat 1/2 of the oil in wok; stir-fry peanuts until browned lightly. Remove from wok; drain on absorbent paper.

• Stir-fry breadcrumb mixture in same wok until browned lightly.

• Add noodles to wok; stir-fry until noodles are hot. Remove noodle mixture from wok; cover to keep warm.

• Heat remaining oil in same wok; stir-fry the artichokes, onion, chilli and olives, in batches, until onion is browned lightly.

• Return artichoke mixture to wok with sauce and stock; stir-fry, tossing until sauce boils.

• Serve artichoke mixture gently tossed with fried noodles and peanuts.

SERVES 4 TO 6

Left Athenian lamb, fetta and artichokes
Right Artichokes with fried noodles and peanuts

THE SULTAN'S LAMB

1/2 cup (125ml) lemon juice
1/3 cup chopped fresh
   coriander leaves
1/4 cup (60ml) olive oil
2 teaspoons ground cumin
2 teaspoons sweet paprika
3 bird's-eye chillies, seeded,
   chopped finely
1 large (300g) red onion,
   chopped finely
3 cloves garlic, crushed
1kg lamb eye of loin, sliced thinly
2 tablespoons peanut oil
2 medium (300g) brown
   onions, sliced
1/2 cup (70g) slivered
   almonds, toasted
1 1/2 cups (250g) seeded
   prunes, halved
1/4 cup (60ml) beef stock

COUSCOUS
1 tablespoon olive oil
2 cloves garlic, crushed
2 teaspoons ground cumin
1 teaspoon ground cardamom
2 1/4 cups (450g) couscous
2 1/4 cups (560ml) beef stock

• Combine juice, coriander, olive oil,
cumin, paprika, chilli, 1/2 of the red
onion, garlic and lamb in large bowl,
cover; refrigerate 3 hours or overnight.

To cook Heat peanut oil in wok; stir-fry
lamb mixture and brown onion, in
batches, until lamb is browned.

• Return lamb mixture to wok with
almonds, prunes and stock; stir-fry,
tossing until sauce boils.

• Serve lamb with Couscous.

Couscous Heat oil in medium pan, add
garlic, remaining red onion, cumin and
cardamom; cook, stirring, until onion is
soft. Stir in couscous and hot stock;
remove from heat, stand, covered,
5 minutes or until stock is absorbed.
Use fork to stir through couscous to
separate grains.

SERVES 6

FULL O' FLAVOUR LAMB AND GREEN BEANS

700g lamb eye of loin, sliced thinly
1 tablespoon ground cumin
1 tablespoon ground coriander
1 tablespoon garlic salt
1 tablespoon mustard powder
2 teaspoons ground fennel
1/3 cup (80ml) peanut oil
450g baby green beans
1 medium (150g) brown
   onion, sliced
30g butter
1 clove garlic, crushed
1/3 cup finely chopped fresh chives

• Combine lamb, cumin, coriander, garlic,
salt, mustard, fennel and 1/2 of the oil in
large bowl; cover; refrigerate lamb
mixture 3 hours or overnight.

To cook Boil, steam or microwave beans
until almost tender; drain.

• Heat remaining oil in wok; stir-fry lamb
and onion, in batches, until browned.

• Heat butter in same wok; stir-fry beans
and garlic until beans are hot.

• Serve lamb mixture and beans sprinkled
with chives.

SERVES 4 TO 6

Platter and bowl from Made in Japan; chopsticks from Dinosaur Designs

Left The sultan's lamb
Right Full o' flavour lamb and green beans

CHICKEN TUSCANY

700g single chicken breast fillets,
sliced thinly
1/2 teaspoon sweet paprika
1/4 cup (60ml) olive oil
2 medium (300g) brown
onions, sliced
3 cloves garlic, crushed
2 medium (380g) tomatoes,
seeded, sliced
1 tablespoon drained capers
2 tablespoons tomato paste
1/4 cup (60ml) dry white wine
1/4 cup (60ml) chicken stock
500g frozen broad beans,
cooked, peeled
1/4 cup firmly packed fresh
basil leaves
1/3 cup (90g) black olive paste
1/3 cup (25g) flaked
parmesan cheese

• Combine chicken with the paprika in
large bowl.

• Heat 1 tablespoon of the oil in wok;
stir-fry chicken, onion and garlic, in
batches, until chicken is browned and
cooked through.

• Heat remaining oil in wok; stir-fry
tomato and capers until tender.

• Return chicken to wok with combined
paste, wine and stock; stir-fry until
sauce boils.

• Add broad beans and basil to wok; stir-
fry, tossing until hot.

• Serve chicken mixture topped with olive
paste and cheese.

SERVES 4

LAMB PROVENÇALE

700g lamb eye of loin, sliced thinly
1/4 cup (60ml) olive oil
2 tablespoons lemon juice
2 cloves garlic, crushed
1 medium (150g) brown
onion, sliced
1 medium (200g) green
capsicum, chopped
2 medium (240g) zucchini, chopped
2 baby (120g) eggplants, chopped
1 cup (250ml) tomato juice
2 medium (380g) tomatoes,
seeded, sliced
1 tablespoon chopped fresh oregano

• Combine lamb, 1 tablespoon of the oil,
lemon juice and garlic in large bowl,
cover; refrigerate 3 hours or overnight.

To cook Heat remaining oil in wok;
stir-fry lamb and onion, in batches,
until lamb is browned.

• Stir-fry capsicum, zucchini and eggplant in same wok until tender.

• Return lamb to wok with tomato juice,
tomato and oregano; stir-fry, tossing
until juice boils.

SERVES 4

Above Chicken Tuscany
Right Lamb provençale

SQUID WITH LIME-CAPER BUTTER

800g squid hoods
2 teaspoons finely grated lime rind
2 cloves garlic, crushed
1 tablespoon chopped fresh parsley
1 tablespoon olive oil
60g butter, melted
1/4 cup (60ml) lime juice
1 tablespoon Dijon mustard
1 teaspoon sugar
1 tablespoon drained baby capers
240g curly endive

• Cut squid hoods in half; score shallow criss-cross pattern on inside surface, cut into 3cm pieces. Combine squid with rind, garlic and parsley in large bowl, cover; refrigerate 3 hours or overnight.

To cook Heat oil in wok; stir-fry squid, in batches, until browned and tender.

• Return squid to wok with combined butter, juice, mustard, sugar and capers; stir-fry, tossing until sauce boils.

• Serve squid over curly endive.

SERVES 4

CAJUN LEMON CHICKEN

700g chicken tenderloins, sliced
2 tablespoons Cajun Seasoning
2 tablespoons peanut oil
1 medium (170g) red onion, sliced
1 medium (200g) red
    capsicum, sliced
1 medium (200g) green
    capsicum, sliced
1 medium (200g) yellow
    capsicum, sliced
2 tablespoons cornflour
1/2 cup (125ml) lemon juice
3/4 cup (180ml) water
1/4 cup (55g) sugar
40g butter

• Combine chicken with the Seasoning in large bowl.

• Heat oil in wok; stir-fry chicken and onion, in batches, until chicken is browned and cooked through.

• Stir-fry capsicum in same wok until just tender; remove from wok.

• Add blended cornflour and juice, to same wok with water, sugar and butter; stir-fry until sauce boils.

• Return chicken mixture and capsicum to wok; stir-fry, tossing until coated in sauce.

SERVES 4

Left Squid with lime-caper butter
Right Cajun lemon chicken

LAMB WITH CHICKPEAS AND SILVERBEET

700g lamb fillets, sliced thinly
2 cloves garlic, crushed
1 tablespoon ground cumin
1 tablespoon ground coriander
2 teaspoons chilli powder
¼ cup (60ml) peanut oil
1 tablespoon grated lemon rind
1 medium (150g) brown onion,
chopped finely
1 medium (200g) red capsicum,
sliced thinly
425g can chickpeas, rinsed, drained
⅓ cup (80ml) lemon juice
500g silverbeet, trimmed, chopped

• Combine lamb, garlic, cumin, coriander, chilli, 1 tablespoon of the oil and rind in large bowl, cover; refrigerate lamb mixture 3 hours or overnight.

To cook Heat remaining oil in wok; stir-fry lamb mixture and onion, in batches, until lamb is browned.

• Stir-fry capsicum in wok until tender.

• Return lamb mixture to wok with chickpeas and juice; stir-fry, tossing until combined. Place in serving dish; wipe wok clean with absorbent paper.

• Stir-fry silverbeet in same wok, tossing until just crisp; serve with lamb mixture.

SERVES 4

MIXED MUSHROOMS IN GARLIC BUTTER

400g field mushrooms
2 tablespoons peanut oil
1 large (200g) brown onion, sliced
2 cloves garlic, crushed
400g Swiss brown mushrooms
400g button mushrooms
2 teaspoons garlic salt
100g butter

• Quarter field mushrooms.

• Heat oil in wok; stir-fry onion, garlic and all mushrooms, in batches, until tender.

• Return mushrooms to wok with garlic salt and chopped butter; stir-fry until butter is melted. Serve on toast, sprinkled with baby basil leaves, if desired.

SERVES 4

Left Lamb with chickpeas and silverbeet
Right Mixed mushrooms in garlic butter

GREEK MUSSEL SALAD

1kg small black mussels
3 medium (570g) tomatoes
2 teaspoons olive oil
1 medium (150g) brown onion,
  chopped finely
2 cloves garlic, crushed
1/4 cup finely chopped
  fresh oregano
1 tablespoon tomato paste
1/2 cup (125ml) water
1 1/2 cups (180g) seeded
  black olives
175g fetta cheese, crumbled

• Scrub mussels, remove beards.

• Halve tomatoes; remove and reserve seeds and pulp, slice tomato flesh.

• Heat oil in wok; stir-fry onion and garlic until onion is soft.

• Add mussels to wok with reserved tomato seeds and pulp, 2 tablespoons of the oregano, tomato paste and the water; stir until sauce boils and mussels open (discard any that do not).

• Combine mussel mixture in large bowl with olives, cheese and reserved tomato flesh; sprinkle with remaining oregano.

SERVES 4

MEDITERRANEAN CHICKEN SAUSAGES

12 thin (840g) chicken sausages
1 tablespoon olive oil
1 large (200g) white onion, sliced
1 clove garlic, crushed
4 baby (240g) eggplants, sliced
2 medium (240g) zucchini, sliced
250g cherry tomatoes
1/4 cup chopped fresh basil leaves
1/4 cup (20g) flaked
  parmesan cheese

• Cook sausages in large pan of boiling water, uncovered, 5 minutes; drain, cut in thin slices.

• Heat oil in wok; stir-fry sausage, onion and garlic, in batches, until sausage is browned and cooked through.

• Stir-fry eggplant and zucchini in same wok until vegetables are just tender.

• Return sausage mixture to wok with tomatoes; stir-fry, tossing until combined.

• Serve sausage mixture, tossing basil through off the heat, with the cheese sprinkled over the top.

SERVES 4

Left Greek mussel salad
Right Mediterranean chicken sausages

PORK, PASSIONFRUIT AND PISTACHIOS

You need about 6 passionfruit for this recipe.

1kg pork fillets, sliced thinly
1/2 cup (125ml) passionfruit pulp
4 bird's-eye chillies, seeded,
    chopped finely
3 cloves garlic, crushed
2 teaspoons raw sugar
250g rice stick noodles
2 tablespoons peanut oil
2 medium (340g) red onions, sliced
3/4 cup (105g) shelled
    pistachios, toasted
1 cup (170g) raisins
1/4 cup (60ml) chicken stock

• Combine pork, passionfruit, chilli, garlic and sugar in large bowl, cover; refrigerate 3 hours or overnight.

To cook Place noodles in medium heatproof bowl, cover with boiling water, stand until just tender; drain.

• Heat oil in wok; stir-fry pork mixture and onion, in batches, until pork is browned and cooked through.

• Return pork mixture to wok with reserved marinade, noodles and remaining ingredients; stir-fry, tossing until sauce boils.

SERVES 6

SPICE-SCENTED BEEF, APPLES AND PRUNES

1kg beef steak, sliced thinly
2 teaspoons ground cinnamon
2 teaspoons ground cloves
2 tablespoons brown sugar
3 cloves garlic, crushed
1/4 cup chopped fresh chives
1/3 cup (80ml) peanut oil
2 small (200g) red onions,
    sliced thinly
2 medium (300g) red apples,
    unpeeled, grated coarsely
1 1/3 cups (225g) seeded
    prunes, halved

• Combine beef, cinnamon, cloves, sugar, garlic, chives and 1/2 of the oil in large bowl, cover; refrigerate 3 hours or overnight.

To cook Heat remaining oil in wok; stir-fry beef mixture and onion, in batches, until beef is browned.

• Return beef mixture to wok with apple and prunes, stir-fry, tossing to combine all ingredients.

SERVES 4 TO 6

Left Pork, passionfruit and pistachios
Right Spice-scented beef, apples and prunes

GLOSSARY

chinese cabbage

baby bok choy

bok choy

choy sum

tat soi

chinese water spinach

ARTICHOKE HEARTS tender centre of the globe artichoke, itself the large flower-bud of a member of the thistle family; having tough petal-like leaves, edible in part when cooked. Artichoke hearts can be harvested fresh from the plant or purchased canned or in brine in glass jars.

BACON RASHERS also known as slices of bacon; made from pork side, cured and smoked. Streaky bacon is the fatty end of a bacon rasher (slice), without the lean (eye) meat.

BAMBOO SHOOTS the tender young shoots of bamboo plants, available fresh from Asian food stores or specialty greengrocers, or canned.

BARBECUE SAUCE a spicy, tomato-based sauce used to marinate or baste, or as an accompaniment.

BEANS
Borlotti also known as Roman beans, these dried beans are also frequently used as a substitute for pinto beans because of the similarity in appearance – both are pale pink with darker red spots. They can be used for Mexican *frijoles refritos* (refried beans), and in soups and salads.
Broad also known as fava beans, these are available fresh, canned and frozen. These are best peeled twice, discarding both the outer long green pod and sandy-green tough inner shell.
Butter another name for lima beans, sold both dried and canned;

curry leaves

kaffir lime leaves

a large beige bean having a mealy texture and mild taste.
Cannellini small, dried white bean similar in appearance and flavour to great northern and navy or haricot beans.
Kidney medium-size dried red bean having a floury yet full flavour; used in soups and stews, and sometimes substituted in Mexican food for borlotti beans.
Snake fresh green beans also called yard-long beans because of their length; used frequently in Asian stir-fries.

BEEF STEAK term used in this book to describe tender, lean beef best for stir-frying:

fillet and rump are first choice; blade, rib-eye (scotch fillet), round and sirloin steak are also suitable but not quite as tender.

BEETROOT also known as garden beets, red beets or, simply, beets; a hard, round, sweet root vegetable that is highly nutritious. Most frequently cooked and eaten pureed, sliced, julienned, etc, but is good eaten raw and dressed in salads.

BLACK BEANS are salted, fermented and dried soy beans. Soak, drain and rinse dried beans; chop before, or mash during cooking to release flavour. **Black bean sauce** is a Chinese sauce made from fermented soy beans, spices, water and wheat flour, and is much used in stir-fry cooking.

BLUE-EYE also known as deep sea trevalla or trevally and blue-eyed cod; thick, moist, white-fleshed fish.

BOK CHOY also called pak choi or Chinese white cabbage; has a fresh, mild

mustard taste and is good braised or in stir-fries. **Baby bok choy**, frequently used in this book, is tender and more delicate in flavour.

BREADCRUMBS
Packaged fine-textured, crunchy, purchased, white breadcrumbs.
Stale 1- or 2-day-old bread made into crumbs by grating, blending or processing.

BURGHUL also known as bulghur wheat; hulled steamed wheat kernels which, once dried, are crushed into various size grains. Used in Middle-Eastern dishes such as kibbeh and taboulleh.

CABBAGE, CHINESE also known as Peking cabbage or Napa cabbage; resembles a cos lettuce in appearance but its taste is similar to the common round cabbage.

CAJUN SEASONING a blend of paprika, basil, onion, fennel, thyme, cayenne and white pepper; used in the Deep South (USA) style of cooking.

CAPSICUM also known as bell pepper, available in red, green, yellow and deep-purple varieties, each with a distinctive taste. Seeds and membranes should be discarded before use.

CHICKEN TENDERLOIN thin strip of tender, succulent meat lying just under the breast; especially good for stir-fry cooking.

CHICKPEAS also called garbanzos, an irregularly round, sandy-coloured legume used extensively in Mediterranean and Hispanic cooking.

CHILLIES available in many different types both fresh and dried. Use rubber gloves when seeding and chopping fresh chillies as they can burn your skin. Removing seeds and membranes lessens the heat level.

CHINESE COOKING WINE a clear distillation of fermented rice, water and salt, about 29.5% alcohol by volume; used for marinades and as a sauce ingredient.

wonton wrappers

gow gee wrappers

CHINESE WATER SPINACH also known as swamp spinach, long green, ung choy and kang kong; leafy green vegetable readily available from Asian specialty shops

CHIPOLATA SAUSAGES, BEEF also known as "little fingers"; highly spiced, coarse-textured sausage.

CHORIZO SAUSAGE Spanish in origin, a highly seasoned spicy salami made from coarsely ground pork, garlic and red peppers.

CHOY SUM also known as flowering bok choy or flowering white cabbage.

COCONUT
Cream available in cans and cartons; as a rule, the proportions are 4 parts coconut to 1 part water.
Milk pure, unsweetened coconut milk available in cans and cartons; as a rule, the proportions are 2 parts coconut to 1 part water.

CORNFLOUR also known as cornstarch; used as a thickening agent in cooking.

COUSCOUS a fine, grain-like cereal product, originally from North Africa, made from semolina, rolled into balls.

CREAM
Fresh (minimum fat content 35%): also known as pure cream and pouring cream; has no additives like commercially thickened cream.
Sour (minimum fat content 35%): a thick, commercially-cultured soured cream good for dips, toppings and desserts such as baked cheesecakes.

CUCUMBER, LEBANESE slender and thin-skinned; also known as the European or burpless cucumber.

CURLY ENDIVE also known as frisee; a curly-leafed green vegetable, mainly used in salads.

CURRY LEAVES shiny bright-green, sharp-ended green leaves used, fresh or dried, in cooking, especially in Indian curries.

EGGPLANT also known as aubergine.

FENNEL also known as finocchio or anise; eaten raw in salads, or braised or fried as a vegetable accompaniment. Also the name given to the dried seeds used in cooking to impart licorice flavour.

FISH FILLETS fresh, firm, white fish pieces sold boned and skinned.

FISH SAUCE also called nam pla or nuoc nam; made from pulverised salted fermented fish, most often anchovies. Has a pungent smell and strong taste; use sparingly. There are many kinds, of varying intensity.

FIVE-SPICE POWDER a fragrant mixture of ground cinnamon, cloves, star anise, Sichuan pepper and fennel seeds.

FLOUR, PLAIN an all-purpose flour, made from wheat.

GARAM MASALA a blend of spices, originating in North India; based on varying proportions of cardamom, cinnamon, cloves, coriander, fennel and cumin, roasted and ground together. Black pepper and chilli can be added for a hotter version.

GHEE clarified butter; with the milk solids removed, this fat can be heated to a high temperature without burning.

GINGER
Fresh also known as green or root ginger; the thick, gnarled root of a tropical plant. Can be kept, peeled, covered with dry sherry in a jar and refrigerated, or frozen in an airtight container.

GOW GEE PASTRY wonton wrappers, spring roll or egg pastry sheets can be substituted in cooking.

HERBS when specified, we used dried (not ground) herbs in the proportion of 1:4 for fresh herbs; eg, 1 teaspoon dried herbs equals 4 teaspoons (1 tablespoon) chopped fresh herbs.

HOISIN SAUCE a thick, sweet and spicy Chinese paste made from salted fermented soy beans, onions and garlic; used as a marinade or baste, or to accent stir-fries and barbecued or roasted foods.

HUMMUS a Middle-Eastern dip made of crushed chickpeas, tahini, garlic and lemon juice.

KAFFIR LIME LEAVES aromatic leaves of a small citrus tree bearing a wrinkled-skinned yellow-green fruit originally grown in South Africa and Southeast Asia.

kumara

KUMARA Polynesian name of orange-fleshed sweet potato often confused with yam.

LAMB
Fry lamb liver.
Eye of loin a cut derived from a row of loin chops; once the bone and fat are removed, the larger portion of remaining meat is referred to as the eye of loin.
Fillet tenderloin the smaller piece of meat from a row of loin chops or cutlets.

LEMON GRASS a tall, clumping, lemon-smelling and tasting, sharp-edged grass used as a herb; the white lower part of each stem is chopped and used in many Asian cuisines or for herbal tea.

LEMON PEPPER SEASONING a blend of crushed black pepper, lemon, herbs and spices.

MAPLE SYRUP distilled sap of the maple tree. Maple-flavoured syrup or pancake syrup is made from cane sugar and artificial maple flavouring and is not an adequate substitute for the real thing.

snow peas

snow pea sprouts

sugar snap peas

bean sprouts

MESCLUN often known as mixed small leaves; consists of an assortment of various edible greens and flowers.

MINCE MEAT also known as ground meat, as in beef, pork, lamb and veal.

MIRIN a sweet low-alcohol rice wine used in Japanese cooking; not to be confused with *sake*, the Japanese rice wine made for drinking.

MIXED SPICE a blend of ground spices usually consisting of cinnamon, allspice and nutmeg.

NOODLES
Bean thread also called cellophane; made from green mung bean flour. Good softened in soups and salads or deep-fried and served with vegetables.
Fresh egg made from wheat flour and eggs; sold in strands varying in thickness.
Fresh rice thick, wide, almost white in colour; made from rice and vegetable oil. Must be covered with boiling water to remove starch and excess oil before using in soups and stir-fries.
Hokkien also known as stir-fry noodles; fresh wheat flour noodles resembling thick, yellow-brown spaghetti needing no pre-cooking before use.
Instant also known as 2-minute noodles; small packages of quick-cooking noodles with flavour sachet.
Rice vermicelli also known as rice-flour noodles; made from ground rice, dried and best used either deep-fried or soaked, then tossed in a stir-fry or stirred into a soup.
Soba thin Japanese noodles made from buckwheat flour and varying proportions of wheat flour.

NORI a type of dried seaweed used in Japanese cooking as a flavouring, garnish or as an ingredient. Sold in thin sheets; some come available already roasted, ready to roll as sushi.

OIL
Olive Extra-virgin and **virgin** are the highest quality olive oils, obtained from the first pressings of tree-ripened olives. Especially good in salad dressings and as an ingredient. **Extra light** or **Light** describes the mild flavour, not the fat levels.
Peanut pressed from ground peanuts; most commonly used oil in Asian cooking because of its high smoke point.
Sesame made from roasted, crushed, white sesame seeds; a flavouring rather than a cooking medium.
Vegetable any of a number of oils sourced from plants rather than animal fats.

ONION
Green also known as scallion or (incorrectly) shallot; an immature onion picked before the bulb has formed, having a long, bright-green edible stalk.
Red also known as Spanish, red Spanish or Bermuda onion; a sweet-flavoured, large, purple-red onion that is particularly good eaten raw in salads.
Spring has crisp, narrow green-leafed top and a fairly large sweet white bulb.

OYSTER SAUCE Asian in origin, this rich, brown sauce is made from oysters and their brine, cooked with salt and soy sauce, and thickened with starches.

PANCETTA an Italian salt-cured pork roll, usually cut from the belly; used, chopped, in cooked dishes mainly to add flavour. Bacon can be substituted.

PASSIONFRUIT also known as granadilla; a tropical fruit native to Australia and South America, comprised of a tough outer skin surrounding edible black sweet-sour seeds.

PLUM SAUCE a thick, sweet and sour dipping sauce made from plums, vinegar, sugar, chillies and spices.

PORK
Chinese barbecued also known as char siew. Traditionally cooked in special ovens, this pork has a sweet-sticky coating made from soy sauce, five-spice and hoisin sauce. It is available ready-to-eat from Asian food stores.
Fillet skinless boneless eye-fillet cut from the loin.
Spareribs thin, long cuts of fatty meat from the lower portion of a pig's rib-section and breast area.

POTATO
Baby new also known as chats. Not a particular type of potato but simply an early harvest.
Kipfler finger-length, light-brown skinned, nutty flavoured potato, good baked or in salads.

red onion

brown onion

white onion

spring onion

green onion

PRAWNS also known as shrimp.

PROSCIUTTO salted-cured, air-dried (unsmoked), pressed ham; usually sold in paper-thin slices, ready to eat, and especially good with melon.

PRUNES commercially- or sun-dried plums.

PUMPKIN sometimes used interchangably with the word squash, the pumpkin is a member of the same family as cucumbers and goards.

ROCKET also known as arugula, rugula and rucola; a green salad leaf having a sharp, peppery taste.

SAFFRON stigma of a member of the crocus family, available in strands or ground form; imparts a yellow-orange colour to food once infused. The most expensive spice in the world; remains fresh longer if kept under refrigeration.

SAMBAL OELEK (also ulek or olek) Indonesian in origin; a salty paste made from ground chillies, vinegar and various spices.

SESAME SEEDS black and white are the most common of the oval seeds harvested from the tropical plant *Sesamum indicum*; however, there are red and brown varieties also. Used in za'atar, halva and tahini. To toast, spread seeds evenly in non-stick pan, stir over moderate heat briefly.

SICHUAN PEPPERCORNS also known as Chinese pepper; small, red-brown seeds resembling black peppercorns having a peppery-lemon flavour.

SNOW PEAS also called mange tout ("eat all").

soba

rice vermicelli

2-minute noodles

rice-stick noodles

bean thread noodles

thick egg noodles

hokkien noodles

rice noodles

thin egg noodles

SOY SAUCE made from fermented soy beans. Several variations are available in most supermarkets and Asian food stores.
Ketjap manis Indonesian sweet, thick soy sauce which has sugar and spices added.
Light as the name suggests, light in colour. It is lighter in density than regular soy but is generally quite salty.

SPINACH
Leaves, baby also known as baby English spinach leaves; delicate green leaves on thin stems. High in iron, good eaten raw or just wilted. The green vegetable often called spinach is in fact **silverbeet**, also known as seakale or Swiss chard, a bigger, stronger-flavoured green-leafed vegetable.

SPROUTS
Bean also known as bean shoots; tender new growths of assorted beans and seeds germinated for consumption as sprouts. The most readily available are mung bean, soy bean, alfalfa and snow pea sprouts.

STAR ANISE a dried star-shaped pod whose seeds have an astringent aniseed flavour.

STOCK 1 cup (250ml) stock is the equivalent of 1 cup (250ml) water plus 1 crumbled stock cube (or 1 teaspoon stock powder).

SUGAR we used coarse, granulated table sugar, also known as crystal sugar, unless otherwise specified.
Caster also known as superfine or finely granulated table sugar.
Palm very fine sugar from the coconut palm. It is sold in cakes, also known as gula jawa, gula melaka and jaggery. Palm sugar can be substituted with brown or black sugar.

SUGAR SNAP PEAS tiny pods with small, formed peas inside which are eaten whole, cooked or raw.

TABASCO SAUCE brand name of an extremely fiery sauce made from vinegar, hot red peppers and salt.

TACO SAUCE a bottled mixture of chopped tomato, vinegar, chillies and spices.

TAHINI a rich, buttery paste made from crushed sesame seeds; used in making hummus and various Middle-Eastern sauces.

TAMARIND
Thick concentrate a thick, purple-black, ready to use paste extracted from the pulp of the tamarind bean; used as is, with no soaking, stirred into curries for a tart sweet-sour taste.

TANDOORI PASTE consisting of garlic, tamarind, ginger, coriander, chilli and spices.

TAT SOI (rosette pak choy, tai gu choy, Chinese flat cabbage) a tender variety of bok choy, developed to grow close to the ground so it is easily protected from frost.

TOFU also known as bean curd, an off-white, custard-like product made from the "milk" of crushed soy beans; comes fresh as silken, soft or firm, and processed as fried or pressed dried sheets.

VINEGAR
Balsamic authentic only if made from a regional white wine from Modena, Italy.
Raspberry made from fresh raspberries distilled with white wine vinegar.
Rice made from fermented rice and flavoured with sugar and salt. Also known as Seasoned Rice Vinegar.

WASABI an Asian horseradish used to make the pungent, green-coloured sauce traditionally served with Japanese raw fish dishes; sold in powdered or paste form.

WATER CHESTNUTS resemble chestnuts in appearance, hence the name. They are small brown tubers with a crisp, white, nutty-tasting flesh. Best when used fresh, however, canned water chestnuts are more easily obtained and can be kept, under refrigeration, about a month once opened.

WATERCRESS small, crisp, deep-green, rounded leaves having a slightly bitter, peppery flavour. Good in salads and on sandwiches.

WITLOF also known as chicory or Belgian endive; good in salads or cooked, especially with cream.

WONTON WRAPPERS small raw pastry rounds; gow gee, egg or spring roll pastry sheets can be substituted.

ZUCCHINI also known as courgette; green, yellow or grey member of the squash family having edible flowers.

INDEX

MAKE YOUR OWN STOCK

These recipes can be made up to 4 days ahead and stored, covered, in the refrigerator. Be sure to remove any fat from the surface after the cooled stock has been refrigerated overnight. If the stock is to be kept longer, it is best to freeze it in smaller quantities.

Stock is also available in cans or tetra packs. Stock cubes or powder can be used. As a guide, 1 teaspoon of stock powder or 1 small crumbled stock cube mixed with 1 cup (250ml) water will give a fairly strong stock. Be aware of the salt and fat content of stock cubes and powders and prepared stocks.

All stock recipes make about 2.5 litres (10 cups).

BEEF STOCK
2kg meaty beef bones
2 medium (300g) onions
2 sticks celery, chopped
2 medium (250g) carrots, chopped
3 bay leaves
2 teaspoons black peppercorns
5 litres (20 cups) water
3 litres (12 cups) water, extra

Place bones and unpeeled chopped onions in baking dish. Bake in hot oven about 1 hour or until bones and onions are well browned. Transfer bones and onions to large pan, add celery, carrots, bay leaves, peppercorns and water, simmer, uncovered, 3 hours. Add extra water, simmer, uncovered, further 1 hour; strain.

CHICKEN STOCK
2kg chicken bones
2 medium (300g) onions, chopped
2 sticks celery, chopped
2 medium (250g) carrots, chopped
3 bay leaves
2 teaspoons black peppercorns
5 litres (20 cups) water

Combine all ingredients in large pan, simmer, uncovered, 2 hours; strain.

FISH STOCK
1.5kg fish bones
3 litres (12 cups) water
1 medium (150g) onion, chopped
2 sticks celery, chopped
2 bay leaves
1 teaspoon black peppercorns

Combine all ingredients in large pan, simmer, uncovered, 20 minutes; strain.

VEGETABLE STOCK
2 large (360g) carrots, chopped
2 large (360g) parsnips, chopped
4 medium (600g) onions, chopped
12 sticks celery, chopped
4 bay leaves
2 teaspoons black peppercorns
6 litres (24 cups) water

Combine all ingredients in large pan, simmer, uncovered, 1 1/2 hours; strain.

FACTS AND FIGURES

Wherever you live, you'll be able to use our recipes with the help of these easy-to-follow conversions. While these conversions are approximate only, the difference between an exact and the approximate conversion of various liquid and dry measures is but minimal and will not affect your cooking results.

DRY MEASURES

Metric	Imperial
15g	1/2oz
30g	1oz
60g	2oz
90g	3oz
125g	4oz (1/4lb)
155g	5oz
185g	6oz
220g	7oz
250g	8oz (1/2lb)
280g	9oz
315g	10oz
345g	11oz
375g	12oz (3/4lb)
410g	13oz
440g	14oz
470g	15oz
500g	16oz (1lb)
750g	24oz (1 1/2lb)
1kg	32oz (2lb)

LIQUID MEASURES

Metric	Imperial
30ml	1 fluid oz
60ml	2 fluid oz
100ml	3 fluid oz
125ml	4 fluid oz
150ml	5 fluid oz (1/4 pint/1 gill)
190ml	6 fluid oz
250ml	8 fluid oz
300ml	10 fluid oz (1/2 pint)
500ml	16 fluid oz
600ml	20 fluid oz (1 pint)
1000ml (1 litre)	1 3/4 pints

HELPFUL MEASURES

Metric	Imperial
3mm	1/8in
6mm	1/4in
1cm	1/2in
2cm	3/4in
2.5cm	1in
5cm	2in
6cm	2 1/2in
8cm	3in
10cm	4in
13cm	5in
15cm	6in
18cm	7in
20cm	8in
23cm	9in
25cm	10in
28cm	11in
30cm	12in (1ft)

MEASURING EQUIPMENT

The difference between one country's measuring cups and another's is, at most, within a 2 or 3 teaspoon variance. (For the record, 1 Australian metric measuring cup holds approximately 250ml.) The most accurate way of measuring dry ingredients is to weigh them. When measuring liquids, use a clear glass or plastic jug with the metric markings.

If you would like to purchase The Australian Women's Weekly Test Kitchen's metric measuring cups and spoons (as approved by Standards Australia), turn to page 120 for details and order coupon. You will receive:

- a graduated set of 4 cups for measuring dry ingredients, with sizes marked on the cups.
- a graduated set of 4 spoons for measuring dry and liquid ingredients, with amounts marked on the spoons.
- 1 teaspoon: 5ml
- 1 tablespoon: 20ml.

Note: North America and UK use 15ml tablespoons. All cup and spoon measurements are level.

How To Measure

When using graduated metric measuring cups, shake dry ingredients loosely into the appropriate cup. Do not tap the cup on a bench or tightly pack the ingredients unless directed to do so. Level top of measuring cups and measuring spoons with a knife. When measuring liquids, place a clear glass or plastic jug with metric markings on a flat surface to check accuracy at eye level.

We use large eggs having an average weight of 60g.

OVEN TEMPERATURES

These oven temperatures are only a guide. Always check the manufacturer's manual.

	C° (Celsius)	F° (Fahrenheit)	Gas Mark
Very slow	120	250	1
Slow	150	300	2
Moderately slow	160	325	3
Moderate	180 - 190	350 - 375	4
Moderately hot	200 - 210	400 - 425	5
Hot	220 - 230	450 - 475	6
Very hot	240 - 250	500 - 525	7

Looking after your interest...

Keep your Home Library cookbooks clean, tidy and within easy reach
with slipcovers designed to hold up to 12 books. *Plus* you can follow our recipes perfectly
with a set of accurate measuring cups and spoons, as used by the Women's Weekly Test Kitchen

TO ORDER

Mail or fax Photocopy or complete the coupon below and post or
fax to AWW Home Library Reader Offer, ACP Direct, PO Box 7036,
Sydney NSW 1028 or fax to (02) 9267 4363.

Credit cards Have your details ready, Sydney: (02) 9260 0000;
elsewhere in Australia: 1800 252 515
(free call, Mon-Fri, 8.30am-5.30pm).

PRICE

Book Holder $11.95 (Australia);
elsewhere $A21.95.

Metric Measuring Set $5.95
(Australia); $A8.00 (New Zealand);
$A9.95 elsewhere. Prices include
postage and handling.
This offer is available
in all countries.

PAYMENT

Australian residents We accept the credit cards listed, money orders and cheques.

Overseas residents We accept the credit cards listed, drafts in $A drawn on an Australian bank,
and also British, New Zealand and U.S. cheques in the currency of the country of issue.
Credit card charges are at the exchange rate current at the time of payment.

- -

☐ **BOOK HOLDER**　☐ **METRIC MEASURING SET**

Please indicate number(s) required.

Mr/Mrs/Ms _____

Address _____

_____

Postcode _____ Country _____

Ph: Bus. Hours:(　　) _____

I enclose my cheque/money order for $ _____ payable to ACP Direct

OR: please charge my:

☐ Bankcard ☐ Visa ☐ MasterCard ☐ Diners Club ☐ Amex

Expiry Date ____/____

Cardholder's signature _____

*Please allow up to 30 days for delivery within Australia. Allow up to
6 weeks for overseas deliveries. Both offers expire 31/12/99.*
HLSWOK99